26 WORDS
about Faith, Ethics,
and Spirituality

Alphabet of Faith

Sara Jewell

WOOD LAKE

Editor: Mike Schwartzentruber
Proofreader: Dianne Greenslade
Designer: Robert MacDonald

LIBRARY AND ARCHIVES CANADA CATALOGUING IN PUBLICATION
Title: Alphabet of faith : 26 words about faith, ethics, and spirituality / Sara Jewell.
Names: Jewell, Sara, author.
Identifiers: Canadiana (print) 20210313862 | Canadiana (ebook) 20210313943 |
ISBN 9781773435176 (softcover) | ISBN 9781773435183 (HTML)
Subjects: LCSH: Christian life – Miscellanea. | LCSH: Christian ethics – Miscellanea. |
LCSH: Faith – Miscellanea. | LCSH: Spirituality – Miscellanea.
Classification: LCC BV4517 .J49 2021 | DDC 248 – dc23

Copyright © 2021 Sara Jewell
All rights reserved. No part of this publication may be reproduced – except in the case
of brief quotations embodied in critical articles and reviews – stored in an electronic retrieval
system, or transmitted in any form or by any means, electronic, mechanical, photocopying,
recording, or otherwise, without prior written permission of the publisher or copyright holder.

All scripture quotations are used by permission. Scripture quotations marked CEV are from the
Contemporary English Version, copyright © 1991, 1992, 1995 by American Bible Society. Scripture
quotations marked CEB are from the *Common English Bible*, copyright © 2011, Abingdon,
Nashville, TN. Scripture quotations marked NIV are from the *New International Version*,
copyright © 1973, 1974, 1984, by International Bible Society. Used by permission of Zondervan
Publishing House. Scripture quotations marked NRSV are from the *New Revised Standard Version*
of the Bible, copyright © 1946, 1952, and 1971 by the Division of Christian Education of the
National Council of the Churches of Christ in the USA. All rights reserved.
Scripture quotations marked MSG are from *The Message* by Eugene H. Peterson, 1995,
Navpress Publishing Group. Scripture quotations marked NCV are from
the *New Century Version*, copyright © 2005 by Thomas Nelson, Inc.

ISBN 978-1-77343-517-6

Published by Wood Lake Publishing Inc.
485 Beaver Lake Road, Kelowna, BC, Canada v4v 1s5
www.woodlake.com | 250.766.2778

Wood Lake Publishing acknowledges the financial support of the
Government of Canada. Wood Lake Publishing acknowledges the financial support
of the Province of British Columbia through the Book Publishing Tax Credit.

Wood Lake Publishing acknowledges that we operate in the unceded territory of
the Syilx/Okanagan People, and we work to support reconciliation and challenge
the legacies of colonialism. The Syilx/Okanagan territory is a diverse and beautiful
landscape of deserts and lakes, alpine forests and endangered grasslands.
We honour the ancestral stewardship of the Syilx/Okanagan People.

GOLD

Printed in Canada
PRINTING 10 9 8 7 6 5 4 3 2 1

CONTENTS

INTRODUCTION • 7

A IS FOR ACCEPTANCE • 13
B IS FOR BOX • 24
C IS FOR COMFORT • 34
D IS FOR DOUBT • 44
E IS FOR ENERGY • 54
F IS FOR FRIENDSHIP • 63
G IS FOR GRACE • 73
H IS FOR HOUSE • 84
I IS FOR IMAGE OF GOD • 91
J IS FOR JUSTICE • 103
K IS FOR KINGDOM • 112
L IS FOR LIMINAL SPACE • 121
M IS FOR MIRACLE • 131
N IS FOR NOISE • 140
O IS FOR OUTCASTS AND ODDBALLS • 148
P IS FOR PANDEMIC, POVERTY, PRIVILEGE • 158
Q IS FOR QUESTIONS • 167
R IS FOR REST • 175
S IS FOR SEEDS • 182
T IS FOR TIME • 193
U IS FOR UNITY • 200
V IS FOR VISION • 207
W IS FOR WILDERNESS • 213
X IS FOR X MARKS THE SPOT • 222
Y IS FOR YES • 229
Z IS FOR ZEAL • 236

AFTERWORD: WORDS OF FAITH • 244
ACKNOWLEDGMENTS • 253
ABOUT THE AUTHOR • 254

AUTHOR'S NOTE

For this book, I have chosen to use the word "kin-dom" when speaking generally about what Jesus calls the "kingdom" of God, except in *K Is for Kingdom*. The hyphen indicates the missing letter g but also makes the word kin (as in family) stand out.

I do my best to keep track of my sources, but I also read a lot and information gets all swirled up inside my brain. When I sit down to write, it is a free-flow process so if I have inadvertently used a phrase or idea that was not mine without crediting the source, it was not intentional.

INTRODUCTION

*We write, we make music, we draw pictures because
we are listening for meaning, feeling for healing.*
— MADELEINE L'ENGLE

In November 2019, while providing pulpit supply at a United Church of Canada congregation in Sackville, New Brunswick, my brain saw a pattern of words and the ever-vigilant part of my writer's brain that is always on the lookout for ideas whispered, "A, B, C!"

On the drive home to Nova Scotia, I thought about doing the "ABCs of Faith" as a sermon series when I returned to my regular pulpit supply work in January.

A month has four Sundays – sometimes five – so I looked at the calendar and discovered that from January 5 to June 28, 2020, there were exactly 26 Sundays. And there are 26 letters in the alphabet.

Holding my breath, I Googled "alphabet of faith," expecting the Internet to be overflowing with links. Amazingly – shockingly – there were very few mentions of a sermon series based on the entire 26-letter alphabet, and not a single book came up.

It was mine, all mine!

Alphabet of Faith was born.

When I picked up a pen and notebook and started to brainstorm words for each letter, there were plenty to choose from, and not all had to be traditional faith words. My intention was to put a fresh spin on them.

I approach my church work as a journalist, a teacher, and a writer. As someone who trusts her instincts and writes from the heart. As someone who reads widely but is not trained or educated by a theological college. As someone who believes the world needs more Jesus.

Back up a bit. If I haven't attended a theological college, how could I do a 26-Sunday sweep of worship services and messages?

When I worked at the local community newspaper, part of my duties involved updating the church notices. One of the United Churches in our rural area changed the name of their worship leader every week and, since I grew up in the United Church and knew how to put a worship service together and wasn't the least intimidated by the thought of writing a message, I offered to help.

The first service I led happened on Epiphany Sunday, January 6, 2013, and if there was one thing I knew about, it was epiphanies. "Going out not knowing" is a bit of a theme in my life, along with "more enthusiasm than skill."

That's how my work as a lay worship leader has rolled out: by trusting my instincts, with confidence in my creative process and skills, and through amazing grace – along with a lot of enthusiasm. I've been fortunate enough to serve one particular congregation in rural Nova Scotia for an extended period of time, which gave me a chance to explore my faith in a way I've been searching for since I was in my 20s.

In 2019, I completed the Licensed Lay Worship Leadership Program and recently applied to become licensed.

After the worship and praise committee approved my request for a 26-Sunday commitment, I planned out the series, selecting words and scriptures and hymns with the understanding they could change at the last minute. By the end of six months, I'd be grateful for the built-in wiggle room because I needed the holy energy of inspiration when the world as we know it changed dramatically in 2020. After all, we are in the world.

The chosen word of the week informed my choice of scripture and the theme of my message, and I always offered a quick thanks when the word actually appeared in a scripture passage. Even when the world went to hell, the creative process rose to the occasion, thereby proving why faith is important; it gives our lives meaning, it connects us to each other, and it helps us make sense of the chaos, mayhem, and evil that confronts us and wears us down.

I'm all about the Christian scriptures and how they apply to life in the 21st century. I seek the wellspring of hope and inspiration that is Jesus, the wisdom of his words and actions as recorded in the gospels. He is the source of our faith and let's be honest: the world needs more Jesus – more blessings, more kindness, more mercy, more justice, more epiphanies, more seeing the light.

For me as a writer, as a thinker, as a seeker and a doubter, as a non-conformist who embraces change, and as a contemporary progressive Christian, doing a sermon series like "Alphabet of Faith" was a gift. Doing it through the worst of 2020 was a rare gift. I will cherish the experience forever, believing myself to be changed as a person of faith and as a follower of Jesus.

Okay, are you feeling my enthusiasm for this? "Alphabet of Faith" was a satisfying, amazing, and challenging sermon series to create, and I am delighted Wood Lake Publishing matched my enthusiasm for creating a collection of essays based on those sermons. I had three Sundays off during those six months, so the essays for H, R, and S are brand new for this book.

Here is how I introduced the sermon series to my congregation on the first Sunday of January.

Are you ready?
During the season of Advent, we prepared ourselves for the birth of Jesus, and for all the ways the life of Jesus would inspire us and change how we live in the world.

Are you ready?
To take a different, deeper look at the life and teachings of Jesus, and your life, and the work of your faith community?

Are you ready to be challenged?

To help us get ready to become emboldened and enthusiastic and fearless followers of Jesus, let's take a moment to centre ourselves through our breath. Let's create space to feel the ageless wisdom of the scriptures, to be inspired by these ancient stories that, remarkably, still speak to our complicated and complex human existence today.

Inhale a deep breath.
Exhale it slowly.
Now,
are you ready?

A is for Acceptance

One thing is clear to me:
We, as human beings, must be willing to accept
people who are different from ourselves.
— BARBARA JORDAN

When I watch and read the news of my community, and of this country (Canada), and of the United States, and of the rest of the world, I try to remember to ask, "Where is Jesus in this scenario?"
Then I wonder what Jesus would think about what's happening.
And my third thought is (or should be),
What would Jesus want us to do about this?

We know Jesus was Jewish, raised and educated in that culture and religious tradition. The purpose of his ministry was to acknowledge the law of Moses, then declare it obsolete. His purpose was to create a new law, a new covenant that would establish a new kin-dom on earth that would be very different from any of the *kingdoms* – particularly Herod's – that already existed in the world as Jesus knew it.
This new kin-dom would be based on a mere two laws: "Love God and love one another."
Deceptively simple, but incredibly challenging.

These two laws both encapsulated and nullified the laws of Moses.

Move over, Uncle, there's a new kid in town with a new way of doing things.

Since Jesus was very much a "Do as I do" kind of guy,
he showed us how to walk this new way by
rejecting the establishment,
skewering the status quo,
embracing the outcasts,
and lifting up the oppressed.
He was a light shining into dim corners and drawing out those hiding there
because of fear of persecution,
because of relentless rejection,
because of broken hearts that wouldn't heal.

Looking at our beautiful, broken, and brutal world today, it's clear we still need to hear about Jesus.
It's clear we still need to understand how he wanted to transform the world.

"He was in the world," John wrote in the opening chapter of his gospel,
"and the world came into being through him; yet the world did not know him.
He came to what was his own,
and his own people did not accept him.

But to all who received him, who believed in his name, he gave power to become children of God …"
(JOHN 1:10–12, NRSV).

His own people did not accept him.

We don't hear this word a lot in church, but acceptance is a huge part of our Christian faith. It's in everything Jesus asks of us: to love our neighbours, to serve others, to forgive.

To offer a chair at the table to everyone, but mainly to those who don't get invited, who are ignored, or who are gossiped about.
To welcome everyone, not only those who are "just like us" – whatever that means.

One of my early visions of "Jesus in the world today" happened when I was a teenager.
It didn't happen at church; it happened in the news.
In 1987, Diana, Princess of Wales, opened the United Kingdom's first unit dedicated to treating people with HIV and AIDS. At the opening,
she shook the bare hand of a man with AIDS – without wearing a glove.

With that simple act of mercy, Diana challenged the world's irrational fears about HIV/AIDS. She showed us what acceptance looks like, and how it transforms

not just those of us witnessing it
but the person receiving it.
Acceptance is a powerful way to fulfill Jesus' commandment to love one another.

In 2019, writer and human rights advocate Amanda Jetté Knox of Ottawa published her first book, a memoir entitled *Love Lives Here: A Story of Thriving in a Transgender Family*.
It's a story about family and fitting in, about courage, authenticity, and acceptance.
It's a story of love.

I read the book in one day. I couldn't stop reading it, but I also had to put it down and walk the dog in order to process what I was reading, to absorb the story.

Transgender means someone does not identify as the gender they were assigned at birth.

According to Stats Canada, in 2018, about 75,000 Canadians aged 15 and older said that they were transgender. That number includes those who are non-binary
(those whose current gender was not reported exclusively as male or female).
A lot of people struggle to understand, let alone accept, what it means to be transgender,
to have a gender identity or gender expression that differs from the sex they were assigned at birth.

A lot of people want to deny the trans experience, and to deny trans people their human rights, including medical procedures that will allow them to be who they are.
A lot of people claim that someone who is transgender is just confused, misled, looking for attention, sick, a freak, even a danger to the public.

You know the rant: a transgender woman
who wants to use the women's bathroom
is a pervert, or a pedophile.

This fear translates into anger and violence. According to the Human Rights Campaign (the largest LGBQT advocacy group in the U.S.), in 2020, 44 transgender or gender non-conforming people were killed worldwide, and those are just the deaths linked to identity that were reported.

How sure you are of your gender, and of how you want to express that gender?
I know how I feel about being a woman. I am sure of my gender and how I express it.
A person who is trans feels the same way, is just as sure about who they are –
only they have to deal with a body that doesn't match how they feel.

In the book, Knox shares the email she and her partner received from their 11-year-old child one evening:

Please don't be angry.
Please try to understand.
I am a girl trapped in a boy's body.
More than anything, I want to be a girl.
Please help me.

Where is Jesus in this story?

Jesus is in that child's room, sitting cross-legged on their bed, encouraging them as they type, braving them up by telling them no matter how anyone else reacts, they are fine just the way they are, they are loved and worthy of love, not as they were born but as the person they are – whoever that person is.

If there's one thing I believe, it's that Jesus –
who commanded us to love each other –
would not turn his back on a person who is trying
bravely and resolutely
to be their true selves.
To be authentic.

If there is one thing we can do for each other, and for the world,
it would be to embrace acceptance.
And not our kind of reserved, conditional,
judgy acceptance
but full-blown radical acceptance –
the kind Jesus calls us to.

One way is to open our minds to the experiences of others, whether we are reading their story or listening to it.

I didn't think I needed to read Knox's book –
after all, I'm an open and accepting person, right? –
then I thought about a young friend of mine from my small rural community
who is walking this road of authentic self,
so I read it because of him.
Turns out, I needed to read this book not because I wasn't open and accepting,
but because I didn't really get my friend's experience.
Now I truly understand what it means to be trans,
to be told you are one gender yet feel like another.
Now I truly understand why names and pronouns matter so much.
More significantly, now I truly understand what acceptance means to a trans person.

In a chapter entitled "Affirmation," Knox writes, "The trans community has one of the highest rates of suicide of any marginalized group. There are many reasons for this, but most can be boiled down to one truth: society treats trans people terribly. A big part of that awfulness is a refusal to believe trans people are who they say they are."

Wait a minute – Jesus was treated in a similar way.
No one believed he was who he said he was.
His own people did not accept him.

They became afraid of how he wanted to change their minds and hearts,
and their way of living and interacting with others.
Their way of benefitting from the established system of beliefs and structure of power.

He was killed because people felt threatened,
rather than inspired.

Jesus wanted to transform us, and our hearts,
to make us more compassionate, more merciful,
more accepting.
He definitely wanted us to be less judgy.
He definitely wanted us to ask, "What if this was *you*? Or your child? Or your grandchild?
Does someone deserve to die for being who they are?"

And we don't like that.
We don't like being challenged like that.
We don't like being told what to do.
We certainly don't like being told what to do by *Jesus*.
How dare he?

My favourite story from Knox's book describes why she decided not to confront an overtly religious mother at her child's school after her child came out as trans.
"I thought I would help her be more like Jesus, who seemed to be a guy she really looked up to. What would Jesus do? Well, if my Catholic school upbringing taught me any-

thing, it's that the man had no issues hanging out with people his daddy considered sinners."

Ah, yes, what would Jesus do?
Be gently in your face.
Hang around until you get to know him.
Make you lose your fear by simply being present.
Serve chocolate chip cookies and grin as you actually enjoyed them and forgot why you didn't want to accept those cookies from him in the first place.

In the end, that mother transferred her children to another school because she could not accept a trans child nor the mother who supported that child.
She was a religious woman who was incapable
of acceptance.
Her mind remained closed.

On the other hand, reading this book made my heart and mind expand,
and I have to tell you, it felt really good to understand.
Understanding is the opposite of fear.
We do better when we know better.
And it's so much easier on our minds and bodies
to accept rather than fear,
to love rather than hate.

Michelle Obama wrote in her 2018 memoir, *Becoming*,
"I've learned it's harder to hate up close."

Michelle made that observation during the 2008 campaign for Barack's nomination as the Democratic Presidential candidate.
She wrote about the way her comments were taken out of context, her shock at how mean people could be,
and about the racism that was a subtle, constant drumbeat.

A page later, she talked about her speech at the Democratic National Convention in the summer of 2008. She said it was findable on YouTube so I put her book down and watched her speech again for the first time since seeing her deliver it live.
About six minutes in, she listed the values both she and Barack were raised with. The third one is this: "You treat people with respect and dignity even if you don't know them, and even if you don't agree with them."

Respect and dignity. That's how we all want to be treated, and we must give in order to receive.
That's the example Jesus gave us, after all.
Respect. Dignity.
Acceptance.

Poet Yung Pueblo wrote,
"Observe. Accept. Release. Transform."

As followers of Jesus, as those commanded to love one another, we know transformation happens when we observe

the lives around us, accept everyone as they are, and release whatever ignorance and fear and judgement we've been holding on to.
We feel our hearts and minds transformed.

Acceptance is empowerment, for every person,
no matter who they are,
and it is through acceptance –
the radical, arms-wide-open kind of acceptance
Jesus asks of us –
that we are empowered to transform the world.

B is for Box

*If you want to know where God is,
find the space in your heart that is open
to all of humankind.*
— SISTER JOAN CHITTISTER

Husband, 8:14 p.m. every night: "You know this is just a TV show, right? You know it's not real?"

Count yourself lucky you don't watch television with me.
Honestly, I'm a nightmare.
I point out plot holes and inconsistencies.
I shout at characters doing things that make no sense.
I melt down when the season finale leaves me hanging.

In 2019, I got mad every time a certain ad for a certain comedy show would come on.

The comedy show in question was the TV series *Miracle Workers*, which cast actor Steve Buscemi as God –
a grizzled, 60-something white man with long, thin grey hair and a scruffy goatee.
Of course, every time I saw the ad, I hollered a phrase we don't say in church.
Because, really?

In the series, God is supposed to be just like us: foolhardy, self-centred, unsophisticated, and definitely not omniscient.
Watching the news, he laments,
"I just feel like packing it all in and moving on to the next thing."
The plot of the show revolves around two low-level angels who try to convince God not to destroy humanity by making a bet with God that they can pull off an impossible miracle: help two humans fall in love.
I realize it's one particular comedy putting its irreverent spin on the near universal Christian-culture concept of God, but every time I see the commercial where grey-haired, grizzled Steve Buscemi says, "I'm God,"
I roar.

Are we really so unimaginative, and so limited, that we can't move past one very particular way of depicting God?

Howard is the name.
Or perhaps, Art, in heaven.

Is it fair to say many of us grew up with God
presented as an old man wearing a flowy white robe
and long, white hair?
After all, Michelangelo immortalized that image in his frescoes on the ceiling of the Sistine Chapel in the early 1500s.
One could argue the painting we know as "The Creation of Adam" has kept God – and us –
shut in a very small box for over 500 years.

That painting offers a very limited and limiting concept of God, especially in light of decades of research into the divine feminine that reveals women were written out of our sacred texts.

Thousands of years ago, the feminine played a much more significant role in human life.
Women were prophets and preachers and healers and revolutionaries,
as well as the life-givers and care-givers.
However, through thousands of years of storytelling,
and story recording,
the roles of women were edited – even edited out.

Sue Monk Kidd explored this in her 1992 book, *The Dance of the Dissident Daughter*.
One of her examples is the "Secret Book of John,"
one of the Gnostic Gospels discovered in a cave in Egypt in 1945,
one of the books rejected from the list of books that eventually made up the Christian scriptures (New Testament).

If there was a deliberate crusade among the early scribes to write women out of sacred texts, no wonder that particular book was tossed.
According to Monk Kidd, John, grieving after the crucifixion, describes the Holy Spirit as female:
"As I was grieving ... a unity in three forms appeared to me, and I marvelled: how can a unity have three forms? ...

It said to me, 'John, why do you doubt? I am the One who is with you always: I am the Father, I am the Mother, I am the Son.'"

Let's see Michelangelo paint that one.

I share this research not to claim God is a woman rather than a man, or even both male and female, but to point out how limiting our way of thinking about God became once we started writing stuff down.
And writing for a particular audience.
And translating words.
And picking and choosing what books and what ideas and what words would be shared with the masses.

Simply by declaring God to be masculine,
and only masculine,
and to be human-esque, and like us,
we totally limited God and our experience with the divine.
We created a very specific box in which to contain God.

In the 20th century, when Christians, particularly in North America, started to read the Bible literally, God's box got even smaller in order to make the divine someone we can control and predict and manipulate.

Dr. David Deane is an associate professor at the Atlantic School of Theology in Halifax. During a conversation with him for a magazine article I was working on, he suggested

one of the reasons Christianity has lost adherents is that we often proclaim a God who is not God:
"We've presented something that isn't convincing, transformative or life-giving, so we deserve to have people fall away from us. I think we need to re-invigorate our doctrine of God and move away from trying to develop a God who can work within the straight-jacket of modern categories."

Believing in a God who grants lottery wins or Super Bowl championships,
or who cures one child's cancer but lets another one die,
is our modern creation of
"a God who is completely cut off from the 'real' world; therefore God is completely irrelevant or God intercedes like a cosmic puppeteer or a cosmic magician,"
said Dr. Deane.

It sounds like reading the Bible literally has brought us to creating a literal God.

According to Dr. Deane, the Bible is "a space where we come to the Word, Jesus Christ, who gives himself to us through the Word, and this encounter changes and shapes us. That's a different kind of encounter than 'this line says this, therefore gay people are going to hell.' It's a different kind of understanding."

By misreading the Bible to suit our needs,
and trying to make God, and the Word, fit our needs,
we put God in a box.
"The God we put in that box is, to my mind, a false idol,"
said Dr. Deane,
"an existing thing rather than a thing who is."

We limited God –

God, who is mystery, who is energy, who is spirit, who is love,
who is the full meal deal with a secret prize inside
that everyone gets whether they want it or not.
Who is in us and between us and around us.
Who is untouchable and unknowable yet who is with us in every moment.
Who is here, there, and everywhere.

Why wouldn't God be male and female, and gay and trans and two-spirited?
Why wouldn't God be no gender at all? Just everyone and each one of us.
Why wouldn't God be a disco ball,
every facet reflecting each of our unique lights at a different angle?

Why can't God just
be?

After all, in the Hebrew scriptures, God is quoted as saying, "I am who I am."
Doesn't get much more open-ended
and inclusive
and expansive
and undefinable as that.
"I am who I am."

An answer full of possibilities.

A God for you, and a God for me.
A God for everyone who believes in love and truth and spirit.

Jesus told the woman from Samaria at the well that "God is spirit, and [God's] worshippers must worship in the Spirit and in truth" (JOHN 4:24, NIV).

When my friend and fellow lay worship leader Lawry MacLeod emailed with some reflections about my message about acceptance, he tapped into the idea of a God who is.
He wrote that if someone asked for help because they were hungry or poor, we'd help,
but when someone asks for help because they are a girl trapped in a boy's body,
we refuse.

"How is this turmoil different from the others?" Lawry asked, then answered:
"Because it's not a physical problem with a simple and temporary solution.
We have to invoke the spirit of God and how it values all human life."

There's a reason why we cling to our labelling, unwelcoming, judgy ways:
Once we change our spiritual attitude of what is acceptable to Jesus,
we can't go back to our old perspective.
It's a new truth, and it means a new way of living and loving.
And we have a deeply ingrained fear of new, different, and inclusive.

As Sarah Bessey, a Canadian Christian author, wrote in the introduction to her memoir, *Miracles and Other Reasonable Things*, "We have to be committed to unlearning the unhelpful, broken, unredemptive, false or incomplete God if we want to have a space to relearn the goodness, the wholeness, the joy of a loving God."

In order to release God from the box we created,
we need to leave the safety and comfort of our own carefully constructed,
impeccably decorated, dust-free and sanitized box.
Why are we afraid to be free?

Why do we prefer to remain in our tight little boxes?

Meister Eckhart, a 14th-century German theologian, once declared,
"God becomes and God unbecomes."

So we can unbecome as well – we can unlearn – because God transcends everything we try to say and write and paint and act.
In truth, God is not something we can understand in our brains,
but rather something we feel in our hearts,
something spiritual that we sense and trust and give ourselves over to,
something in our cells,
in our beats and our breaths and our blinks.
We can't see it, but we can feel it.

Whenever we try to put God in a box, we are simply failing ourselves by limiting our potential.

Instead of trying to make God fit into our small, limited, human-created box, we actually are called to fit into God's box.

And what does God's box look like? What words might describe the box of God?

Huge, borderless, unlimited, love, energetic, holy, sacred, peaceable, infinite, inclusive, expansive, welcoming, whole, universal …

With space for everyone.

That's an amazing and empowering and inspiring box. Well, of course – that's an amazing and empowering and inspiring God.

I am, says God.

C is for Comfort

*Not all of us can do great things, but we can
do small things with great love.*
— MOTHER TERESA

In June 2006, my mother was diagnosed with colon cancer. It was unexpected, as most diagnoses are, and most unwelcome, as most diagnoses are,
but especially since we were six months into my father's residency in the dementia unit at a nursing home, and our days revolved around supporting his care and visiting him every morning and afternoon.

The first step of her treatment was surgery to remove the offending tumour in her colon.
It happened on the Friday before the long weekend of July, and I was scheduled to read the scripture at church that Sunday.
I went ahead with it, and beforehand, I said to my friend Shelagh,
"Wait till you hear it! It's the perfect scripture for me to read."

I don't remember now what it was in that scripture
I referred to

but something completely different tripped me up during my reading.
And I mean, tripped me up.

Three days after my mother had surgery to remove a cancerous polyp,
I had to read the words Jesus spoke to the hemorrhaging woman who touched his robe:
"Daughter, your faith has made you well; go in peace and be healed of your disease"
(MARK 5:34, NRSV).

Now, I choke up pretty easily, especially when speaking about something very meaningful,
but I have never sobbed my way through a message or prayer.
Yep, that's what I did that Sunday in July.
As soon as my brain saw that line and connected it with what was going on in my life,
and with my mother,
I started to cry.
I had no control over my thoughts or my tear ducts.
I cried through the rest of the reading.
No one came to my rescue
so I just kept going to the last verse.

Later, during the Prayers of the People, when a friend of my mother's called out her name,

a ripple of awareness passed through the congregation.
Afterwards, people came up to me and thanked me for
bringing such raw and honest emotion to the reading.
I was mortified, Shelagh laughed, but people *thanked me.*

We forget that church is, and should be, a place where we
can let go and let God.
Where we can get emotional, where we can open our minds
and our hearts,
and express whatever raw and honest emotions
come to us.

We call our traditional gathering space in a church
a sanctuary.
A place of refuge, of safety, of solace.

It is meant to be a place of comfort.
A place where we come to sing and pray and learn, sure,
but where we come to find God in the midst of our lives;
in the midst of our joys but more importantly,
in the midst of our sorrows and sufferings, our heartache
and grief.
In the midst of our letting go.

We show up at church to find comfort
when we are letting go of the burdens we carry:
the guilt, the shame, the regret;
when we are letting go of the negative emotions
we cling to:

anger and resentment and bitterness;
when we are letting go of love:
through the end of a relationship because of distance or
divorce or death.

We show up at church to find comfort because this is supposed to be our community of faith, our faith family, where we are connected to each other based on our beliefs and values, on our history and friendships –
based on what we have in common through Jesus:
the assurance of love, acceptance, welcome,
and no judgement.

Church is that place where everyone is, or should be, welcome.
We say, "Come as you are" and that means:
come when you are happy, come when you are successful,
come when you are celebrating.
But it also should mean more essentially:
come when you are a wreck,
when you are a hot mess,
when you are sad and mourning,
when you are poor and scared,
when you are sick and weak.

That's when we need the comfort of a community
yet church is often the last place we seek out
when we are miserable,
when we are waiting,

when we are lonely,
when we are afraid,
when we are mourning,
because we don't want to get upset.
We don't want to upset others.
We don't want to make a fool of ourselves.

As someone who bawled through an entire scripture reading at the pulpit, I'm totally over worrying about making a fool of myself by showing raw and honest emotion at church.

Here's the interesting part of that: I hadn't cried till then.
Not when my mother was diagnosed,
not when we celebrated her 65th birthday two weeks before her surgery,
not while walking the dog,
not even during final relaxation at the end of a yoga class (and everybody cries then).
I could have cried at any time,
but no moment cracked me open –
until I read that piece of scripture,
until I was with my church friends,
until I was in that sanctuary.

I venture to say it's because,
on some deep, subconscious level,
I felt safe and secure, welcomed and accepted in that space,
with those people.

That if I was going to break down, release my pain and suffering, admit to needing support,
that was the place to do it.
Where I was surrounded by
love and grace and peace and hope.

We go to church not because we feel
the presence of God there –
that's part of it but it's an invisible, intangible, untouchable part.
We go to church –
where we should feel safe and welcome and included,
no matter what state we're in
and what clothes we're wearing –
because we have the actual presence of each other there.
Visible, palpable, touchable people who offer comfort and encouragement.
And tea.
Thank God for hot, dark, church tea.

It's okay to cry through a hymn. It's okay to cry during a Christmas Eve service.
Who doesn't get teary-eyed during a baptism?
Tears of joy and tears of sorrow: every kind of raw and honest emotion should be welcomed
and encouraged in a sanctuary.
Yet over and over, we deny ourselves that healthy release.
We deny ourselves our uniquely human response.
We hold in our emotions,

often by pretending to be strong and in control,
or by avoiding church altogether,
thereby denying ourselves the comfort
that comes from our faith.

Consider, then, that our community of faith offers us not only comfort, but also healing.

In a print interview, historian and New Testament scholar John Dominic Crossan said that anthropologists make a distinction between curing and healing: curing means "eliminating all evidence of disease," while healing means "becoming whole."

You can be healed without being cured.
You can be whole even if you are falling apart.
That happens when you are surrounded by people who love you and care for you,
who support you and help you.
No matter what you are going through.

Healing is about community, but more significantly,
healing is about bringing people into
a new kind of community
where they are not an embarrassment or a burden,
where they are not ignored and excluded,
but where they are welcomed and accepted and supported
to be themselves and live their lives.

This is how we comfort and heal, care for and help.
This is how we are comforted and are cared for.

It was helpful, in fact, to learn this difference because we so often pray for healing,
yet I think of all the people,
including my father who was diagnosed with Alzheimer's disease at the age of 60,
who simply would not be healed
in the cured sense of the word.
Suddenly, the whole healing (and praying) potential of community and faith and love opened up.

Paul wrote to the Philippians, "I can do all things through God who strengthens me,"
so we need to believe we can do all things,
get through all things,
endure all things
through our faith friends who strengthen us.

So this is what I want to say
for whatever level of comfort –
and need to cry –
you are at right now, reading this:

No matter what you have endured so far in life, you have survived.
And the things you have done, gone through, and carried

on in spite of
have transformed you into a better, stronger, wiser version
of you.

Even if you don't feel good, strong, or wise right now.

Everything we fear –
crying, dying, hurting, suffering, waiting, wondering –
becomes something we appreciate and understand
once we've survived it,
and perhaps thrived,
because of it.
We don't fear what we know, so trust in your experience.
Trust in your strength.
Trust in each other.
Because if you need to seek comfort, and have a good cry,
and then keep putting one foot in front of the other,
remember that you aren't alone.
You have friends you can count on,
people who want to help,
people who will heal you with hugs and tea
and ginger cookies,
with walking and listening and feeding you.

People who might actually thank you for making *them* cry
in church.

There is such grace in helping, and in being helped.
In offering comfort and in accepting comfort.
And there is so much grace in providing healing
to everyone who reaches out and touches our robe.

As Jesus said in that reading from Mark
(and let's make it inclusive):
"My friend, by your faith, you are healed. Go in peace."

D IS FOR Doubt

*The whole problem with the world is that
fools and fanatics are always so certain of themselves,
and wiser people so full of doubts.*
— BERTRAND RUSSELL, philosopher and mathematician

Had I known how big a topic doubt would be, and how many versions of my church sermon I would write until I came up with one that was 45 minutes long –
I might have chosen Dog –
as in "Dog is God spelled backwards" –
as my D word.

Much easier to write about unconditional love
and forgiveness,
and not biting the hand that feeds you.

Except that: Doubt is big because it is important.
After all, I'm serving as a lay worship leader because of doubt. Because of the following story from the gospel of Mark in which a father complains to Jesus that the disciples were unable to rid his son of the demon that possessed him (which we now assume was epilepsy).
When the man says to Jesus, "If you can do anything …"
Jesus replies, "'If you can?' All things can be done for the one who believes."

Immediately, the father of the child cried out, "I believe; help my unbelief" (MARK 9:23–24, NRSV).

I believe; help my unbelief – the doubter's mantra.

I believe.
Then, again, I don't know what I believe. Help!

In some ways, having faith and not doubting is easy.
I should have been able to type up three pages very quickly because
we are told not to doubt.
Do not doubt God.
Do not doubt what God says.
Do not doubt what God asks you to do.
Just. Don't. Doubt.

Here's what James said: "Ask in faith, never doubting, for the one who doubts is like a wave of the sea, blown and tossed by the wind" (JAMES 1:6, NRSV).

Be firm in your belief. Be solid. Do not doubt.

Except that … even Jesus doubted.
In the Garden of Gethsemane, before he was arrested, he prayed,
"If it is possible, take this cup of suffering from me"
even as he realized that was not going to happen:
"But it's not what I want but what you want."

How could he not have a moment of doubt about what was coming?
He was, after all, human, and doubts are part of being human.
And yet it's because of doubts –
because of people who question, who ask What if? and Why? and Why not? –
that we live in a completely different world than Jesus did.
We now know so much more
about the universe and this planet,
about our bodies and medicine,
about machinery and technology.
Not to mention just the act of living is very different than in Jesus' time:
Generally speaking,
we survive childbirth, we survive childhood,
we live past the age of 40 – often double that.

Every time some long-standing belief is proven wrong, it gives us a bit of doubt.
What else is wrong?
What else do we not know the truth about?
Are we wrong about God?
Why does everything have to keep changing?

Asking questions and coming up with answers that are different from what other people think, and have been thinking for a long time, expressing doubts and sharing new ideas –

being true to yourself –
takes courage.
Whether it's about something big like religion or something personal like a relationship.
Whether you're changing the layout of the universe or just your major at university.

In a Twitter post, pastor Kevin McGill of Idaho says, "Faith is wrestling with the tension between belief and doubt. It's a willingness to continue to explore, wrestle with difficult questions, and seek true meaning … even if we may never know all the answers."

Doubt is scary.
Doubt rocks our foundation.
Doubt boots us right out of our comfort zone.
Doubt means change.

But if we are brave and we follow our doubts
with integrity and trust in ourselves –
if we believe we have a purpose and are loved –
doubt is freedom.
Doubt is passion and excitement and authenticity.
Doubt opens up our thinking and our feeling.
Doubt expands our world.

Who doesn't want to live like that?
Who doesn't want a faith that makes us feel like that?

Who can follow Jesus and have any doubt we are called to change the world of power and control and greed through kindness and mercy and justice?

For those with inquiring minds,
doubt is the beginning,
not the end,
of faith.

Doubt is the place where we start to find our faith –
a faith we can live out with passion and excitement and authenticity,
a faith that is unique to each of us and our relationship with or experience of the divine.

Doubt helps our beliefs evolve
if we are brave enough to ask,
generation after generation,
century after century,
day in and day out,
"Is this really what God wants?
Is this really what Jesus meant?"

This questioning isn't a way of negating the Word, but rather of exploring it more deeply
and it's these explorations that are leading us to
more acceptance,
more inclusion,
more compassion,

and more kindness.
More Jesus.

Which is rather the point, isn't it?

Let's not overlook, however, the people who stand on a firm foundation of certainty.

Through the Bible, many of us derive great comfort from our faith because it is unchanging and predictable.
Through the Bible, God is knowable and predictable.
We believe today what we believed when we were children, which is what our parents and grandparents believed.

There is a level of comfort in knowing what we know,
in having an unshakeable faith in the validity of the Bible,
in never having any doubts as to the who and what and where and why.
There are those of us who are that certain in our faith, and nothing will change our minds.

That's great.

I'm sure, however, if everyone was honest and open and truthful about what they believed,
each of us would describe a different experience of God, of the gospels, of Jesus.

And we won't all agree with each other – some of us might even be offended.

That's great.

With love, we can contain these multitudes, these diverse experiences, these contrary conversations.
Each of us has a faith
that is as unique and individual as we are.
God is vast enough and mysterious enough and I AM enough to accept and include and welcome everybody.
Even those who start every sentence with, "Yes, but ..."

This is something about which I have no doubt because it's my faith experience.

Theologian Frederick Buechner said,
"Whether your faith is that there is a God or that there is not a God,
if you don't have any doubts, you are either kidding yourself or asleep.
Doubts are the ants in the pants of faith.
They keep it awake and moving."

This is how I've experienced church and God and faith my entire adult life:
My doubts have kept me awake –
at three o'clock in the morning –
and moving

from church to church, searching for something only my heart would recognize.

For heaven's sake, Sara, why can't you just find one place and stick with it?
Have you got ants in your pants?
Why, yes, as it turns out, I do.

Those ants are how I ended up writing about my doubts —
and sharing those doubts in public.
You won't find anyone more uncertain,
more disbelieving,
more doubtful about doing what I do than *me*,
even as I'm doing it.

But I keep showing up,
I keep writing and thinking and sharing
despite those doubts, and *because* of them.

Until I became a lay worship leader, I ignored my doubts.
I stayed away from church
because I wasn't finding any answers,
or even a way of asking any of the questions floating around in my mind.
Doing this work forced me to investigate my doubts,
to ask my questions, to find some answers.

My doubting, my seeking, my exploring —
my willingness to be uncomfortable —

helped me discover something I have complete faith in:
The world needs more Jesus.

For me, doubt has become an act of faith.
It's a path to passion, excitement, and authenticity.

Consider this verse:
"There is no fear in love, but perfect love drives out fear,
because fear expects punishment. The person who is afraid
has not been made perfect in love" (1 JOHN 4:18, CEB).

So if I believe in love,
and in Jesus, and in his ministry and teachings,
if I believe it is possible to doubt AND be faithful –
and not be punished for my doubts, for expressing them –
then what do I have to fear?

Even when you have doubts,
do not fear the journey, do not fear the answer –
because your answers will lead to Jesus,
where you will find love and acceptance and welcome.
You will find more peace and hope and joy
than you expected.
Even at three o'clock in the morning.

Blessed are those who doubt.

As humans, we are evolving and progressing –
in good ways and in bad ways –

and we are always changing.
It's inevitable
that our beliefs and our faith will change, too.
Questions and doubts are a part of living.
The world is changed by those who ask What if? and Why?

Yet I am quite confident, very much without a doubt, in stating the one thing I believe with certainty:
The world needs more Jesus.

E IS FOR Energy

*I will not suck the mystery out of this miraculous
and magical world with my demand to know and
understand everything. I will have faith.
I will rest in the fact that something much bigger
than me is holding this beautiful crap somehow together
and in the end, love wins.*
— LORI HETTEEN, GRAPHIC ARTIST

There is the creative energy that formed the earth.
There is the energy that is the power of the Holy Spirit.
And there is our mental, physical, and spiritual energy.

As humans, we're all energy – electrical and chemical –
and simply by living, by being here, we share our energy.
We exchange energy with everything
with which we interact:
air, earth, trees, birds, bugs, our pets, and of course,
other human beings.

We all know the power of a smile to lighten our spirits,
the power of a good laugh or a good cry
to make us feel better,
the power of enthusiasm and praise
to boost our passion and confidence.
That happens best when we are together –

in the same room, in the same zone –
when my energy mingles with your energy.

Yet so much of human interaction takes place online now, and we're seeing more and more online classes and workshops being offered.
Many of us say it's not the same as being in the same space with other people.

And a virtual hug doesn't carry the exchange of energy, or the power to calm,
that comes with pressing your heartbeat against mine.

Humans aren't robots.
We are thinking, breathing, moving creatures.
We are emotional and spiritual, and we are social.
We need other people because we need their energy to inspire us.
Just think how good a belly laugh with a friend feels.
It's not the same laughing by yourself at a TV show.

Our energy is pretty remarkable –
not only that we have energy as living creatures, but also that there is a part of our energy that, through our faith, connects us to each other and to God.

The essay about the letter C (Comfort) included the story about the hemorrhaging woman who reaches out to touch the hem of Jesus' garment, in order to heal herself.

Jesus felt the power leaving his body.

Even 2,000 years ago,
it appears we had an idea about energy –
that we are connected in some way that we can feel –
and some of us can use that connection, that energy, to help others.
In Jesus' case, it was the power of healing.

We all have at least a minimal power for healing –
remembering that healing isn't curing, but the strengthening of mind and spirit –
and we all have an accessible way of using our energy to help others.

Through touch. Specifically, holding hands.

Holding hands is such a simple gesture, such a quiet way of connecting with someone yet it is very powerful.
We instinctively reach for someone's hand when we are feeling emotion,
when we want to reach out, when we need comforting or want to offer comfort,
when we need to feel secure and connected.
That begins an extraordinary exchange of energy –
it's like we have the power to recharge each other.
I hug you when you're feeling stressed –
suddenly, you feel calmer, and more in control.
You grab my hand when I'm tired, and suddenly –

I'm still tired – but I feel better.
I can do more things through you, who strengthens me.

We need energy – our own and others – in order to live.
Because life isn't easy –
and there are times when that one hand holding ours is all that's holding us together.

Where does our energy for believing, for serving, for loving, for caring come from?

Sunny days, for starters.
Author Annie Dillard said, "There is a muscular energy in sunlight corresponding to the spiritual energy of wind."
Don't we all feel happier when the sun is shining? And when we're outside in nature, going for a walk? Moving and breathing …

Speaking of wind, as Christians, we believe we receive energy from the Holy Spirit.
In our scriptures, the Holy Spirit is often referred to as two different, invisible entities:
wind, blowing gently or with tremendous force, and breath, moving as the life force within each of us.

We can't see the wind, but we can hear it and feel it.
We can't see our breath, but we can hear it and feel it.
We can't really see our energy, our spirit –
but we feel it.

We know all of this is around us, and inside us –
is us – we can feel it but we can't really see it.

Or can we?

We see how energy affects us when we interact with other people.
We encounter the Holy Spirit when we are in relationship.
And we especially encounter energy and Spirit when we show up and offer help.

In her book *Plan B: Further Thoughts on Faith*, author Anne Lamott writes,
"We see the Spirit made visible when people are kind to one another, especially when it's a really busy person like you, taking care of a needy, annoying neurotic person, like you."
When we're willing to let others be their flawed,
imperfect selves,
and accept we are just as flawed and imperfect
as everybody else,
when we are sincere and authentic, no matter what mood anyone is in,
the Holy Spirit will be there –
in us and around us and between us –
bringing us together, giving us what we need
to be kind to each other,
to put up with each other,
to keep showing up for each other.

That takes a lot of energy.
Just the thought of it makes me want to breathe deeply.
Inhale …
Exhale …
Feel better? I bet you do.
We always feel better when we breathe slowly and deeply.

The etymology of the word "inspire" means
"to breathe into" –
and where else do we hope to be inspired by holy energy
than when we are sitting with someone who is going
through a rough time –
who has experienced a loss or a diagnosis
or is in palliative care?

We consider our inspiration "breathed into" us
because Jesus promised that
through the breath – the wind – the energy – of the Spirit,
we would receive the strength and wisdom we need to live
with purpose and joy.

So the exchange of energy that happens when we hug,
when we hold hands,
when we simply sit alongside someone without speaking,
that's all the presence of the Holy Spirit.
That's the power of your holy energy and my holy energy
mingling,
connecting us, comforting us,
empowering us, inspiring us – for whatever we are facing.

I don't know how many times I receive a hug and almost fall into it, I'm so grateful –
so suddenly filled with grace.
"I didn't know I needed a hug!"

The Holy Spirit doesn't just sit there – it has energy, it has purpose –
and it is necessary and of great value.

It's what happens to disciples – then and now.
As if a wind rushes into and around us, we feel an energy and suddenly we are filled with it – filled with an energy that gives us abilities –
to speak, to listen, to create, to sing, to pray –
to be disciples of love and mercy and justice.

This is who we are when we listen to our hearts,
and allow the energy we feel –
the impulse and urges we feel –
to guide us.

I remember a few years into my work as a lay worship leader, wrapping up a service and heading to the back of the church where I waited to greet everyone as they left the sanctuary. As I stood there, listening to the congregation singing their "going out" song
and feeling the kind of feeling
that comes after a worship full of connection,

my eyes filled with tears.
I overflowed with emotion –
and the energy that swirled inside was
spiritual.

The energy I put into that worship – creating it, presenting it – came back to me.
As if it was already there, deep inside me. And I tapped into it through love –
my love of the work, and the congregation's love
of my work.

That's it, in a nutshell.
Love is the energy, deep inside each one of us.
That's who we are.
That's what shows up and keeps us going,
keeps us believing –
I believe, help my unbelief! – every time.
What we feel deep inside us, in our guts, in our hearts
is that universal, infinite and divine energy that connects
us all.

You have it. I have it. Each one of us contains that gift of holy, spiritual energy.

We come from energy and we return to energy.
We are born from Spirit and we return to Spirit.

We are the power of love, the power of light, and the power of grace.
Forever and ever.

F is for Friendship

*Lots of people want to ride with you in the limo
but what you want is someone who will take the bus
with you when the limo breaks down.*
— OPRAH WINFREY

Early in the movie *Bohemian Rhapsody*, the 2018 bio-pic
about Freddie Mercury, the lead singer of the British rock
band Queen, Freddie leaves a club and approaches two
men who played in the band that night.
When Freddie learns the lead singer has just quit,
he says he'd take over because he can write songs
and he can sing.
The drummer laughs –
tells Freddie with teeth like that there's no way
(Freddie Mercury had a remarkable overbite) –
so Freddie turns away, as if to leave.
Then he whips around, opens his mouth,
and belts out their biggest song.
The two men are gobsmacked.

Freddie tells the drummer his teeth give his voice
more range.
They hire him on the spot, and the band Queen is born.

Freddie Mercury, as depicted in the movie, was confident, brash, and brilliant.
He believed in his talent as a singer and as a songwriter, and he pursued it single-mindedly.
But such genius talent often comes with a shadow side: not just the inability to put the needs of others first, but to even see those needs in the first place.

By the middle of the movie, I was aware of something: Freddie needed real friends.
He had his bandmates, but as their fame grew, they chafed at Freddie's exuberant partying
and his disrespect for the work they wanted to do as a band.
He had his fiancé, Mary – until she realized he was gay.
Freddie didn't care; he still wanted her to be his wife – but she couldn't do that. After Mary started a new relationship, the wrong person began influencing Freddie and the choices he made,
yet when he hit rock bottom, it was Mary who pulled him out of the hole. They remained friends for life.
Freddie relied on her
as his rock, as his compass, as well as his best friend.

We all have, or need,
that one friend who keeps us together,
who loves us at our worst, who calls us on our crap –
that one friend who is honest and loyal and loves us just the way we are,
but who won't let us be the worst version of ourselves.

In the fall of 2018, a memory I had suppressed for 25 years
released itself into my conscious mind:
the high school teacher supervising my final practicum
told me that I shouldn't be a teacher.
I never told anyone, not even my best friend, what that
teacher said.
That statement went right into a vault in my brain
locked and inaccessible
until I started substitute teaching and realized
I might have been a really good middle school teacher.

That memory now explains why
I was such a mess in my 20s.
I'd lost the one thing I wanted to do, but because of the
power of the brain to block trauma,
I didn't know what I was doing with my life.
I didn't know why I was unhappy.
I didn't know what I was searching for.
I didn't know that I was unhappy,
didn't know I was searching, didn't know I was lost.

Eventually, my friend Jennifer said to me,
"You're not treating your friends very well."

Some part of me must have known there was something
going on because my reaction at the time wasn't anger –
not even defensive, knee-jerk annoyance –
but rather awe and gratitude that Jennifer had the courage
and the confidence to tell me.

All this talk about friends, and bands,
makes me think of Jesus.
I wonder if he had any friends?

Jesus had a band – maybe you've heard of it?
The Wandering Disciples.
They had a bunch of top ten hits in 30 CE:
"Don't Let Your Hearts Be Troubled"
and "Seek and You Will Find"
and the number one hit, "I Am the Light of the World."
There was Peter on drums, James on guitar, John on bass,
and of course –
Jesus was the lead singer.

Perhaps Jesus was a bit like Freddie Mercury:
Brilliant, focused, charismatic, absolutely devoted to what he believed in –
and totally fixated on what he wanted to accomplish.

And, like Freddie,
Jesus had his own Mary, his own best friend,
who was outside the band,
who could encourage Jesus to be himself and give him a break from all the band stuff,
all the ministering and teaching and travelling,
and playing the new music people were gathering in big crowds to hear –
even as the old folks complained that it was corrupting the young people.

Mary Magdalene – Jesus' best friend.
The one, named in the gospel of John,
who was present for and witness to her friend's death and resurrection.
The disciple whom he loved.

The gospel of John also gives us these words from Jesus:
"Now I tell you to love each other, as I have loved you. The greatest way to show love for friends is to die for them. And you are my friends, if you obey me. Servants don't know what their master is doing, and so I don't speak to you as my servants; I speak to you as my friends"
(JOHN 15:11–15, CEV).
He said this after telling them
all about his friendship with God,
and how it inspired and guided him.

Jesus' life gives us such a picture of friendship,
and how friends become like family,
and the kinds of things that bring us,
and keep us, together,
including those of us who gather in a faith community:
common goals, devotion to a cause, shared beliefs.
Along with those values that sustain
and deepen friendship:
love for one another, trust and loyalty,
honesty and encouragement,
and forgiveness.

In an online article published in 2019, author and pastor Casey Tygrett says,
"There is something *sacramental* about friendships. I'm not ready to create official doctrine about this, but there are times with a close friend where it feels as if you've entered into a tremendous mystery. There is a person who has watched you fail, listened to your confessions, and supported you when no one else would. Despite this, they are still part of your life. They think well of you and enjoy time with you. Still."

That's the kind of friend we seek, isn't it?
The friend who will stick by you, stick with the plan –
who will do anything for you,
even at great cost or sacrifice.

Peter, James, and John could be considered Jesus' closest friends, his "inner circle."
With this trio, Jesus shared his transfiguration, his last supper, and that night in the Garden of Gethsemane,
before he was arrested –
because of Judas' betrayal.

Ah, Judas. Worst friend ever, right?
Or Jesus' BFF?

Judas has always been portrayed as Jesus' betrayer –
but what if it wasn't quite like that?
What if Judas was recast as the betrayer

in the same way Mary Magdalene
was recast as a prostitute?
What if Judas was actually the most courageous of friends because he agreed to fulfill the really big favour Jesus asked of him?

Think about a different friend of Jesus – Thomas, the one always associated with doubt.
Thomas wasn't present when Jesus' made his first post-death appearance to the disciples and Thomas famously said, "Unless I see the nail marks in his hands and put my finger where the nails were, and put my hand into his side, I will not believe it" (JOHN 20:25, NIV).
Apparently, there is a different way of interpreting Thomas' reaction: he wasn't doubting what the others saw; rather, grieving the loss of his beloved teacher and friend, he was upset to have missed it. He just wanted to see Jesus again for himself.

When I read about the discovery and translation of the gospel of Judas (which was found in 2006), I was primed to believe a different story about the man always associated with betrayal.
According to the *National Geographic* translation of the text, rather than portray Judas as Jesus' betrayer, the author of the gospel of Judas called him Jesus' *most favoured* disciple, writing that Jesus asked Judas to betray him to the authorities, so that he could be freed from his physical

body and fulfill what he saw as his destiny of saving humanity.

What would you do for your best friend?
Donate a kidney?
Carry a baby?
Betray him to the authorities so he could be arrested –
thereby making even more of a point than flipping tables in the temple did?

If Jesus was fully aware of what the ancient prophets said,
completely convinced of the truth of his own teachings,
and utterly devoted to seeing his mission
through to the end,
his single-mindedness might have prevented him from considering how his really big favour would affect Judas.
Especially if neither of them honestly thought there was a possibility Jesus –
the most nonviolent of zealots, dedicated to changing the system with words, not swords –
would be crucified.

Maybe the real story of Jesus and Judas isn't one of betrayal,
but of the ultimate devotion and trust of one friend in another.
Perhaps Judas was that one gutsy follower
who was willing to do whatever it took to help Jesus, his friend, achieve

what Jesus saw as his life's purpose,
even if it meant helping him get arrested?

Now, the gospel of Judas was written at least a century after Jesus and Judas died so it's not exactly a reliable source of information – or truth.
My re-imagining of Judas' friendship with Jesus
is merely about giving Judas a chance to be considered differently
than he has always been depicted.
A chance to be redeemed, if only on this page.
We've all had a story told about us that wasn't how we saw ourselves,
that wasn't who we believe we really are – .
and I'm a big fan of redemption stories, of fresh starts and new beginnings.
And where else do we create those stories – and new identities – but with our friends?

In that online article I quoted earlier, Casey Tygrett goes on to say,
"Like any good sacrament, we are brought to the crossroads of God, self, and others in a friendship. In fact, a friendship is a beautiful context for learning how to keep the many and varied commands of Jesus about generosity, forgiveness, and compassion."

We all need that one friend –
a Jennifer, a Mary, maybe even a Judas –

who knows us so well that they know what we need,
and are willing to do anything
to help us become the best version of ourselves.

We all need that friend
who asks hard questions but stays with us as we struggle with the answers,
who sees us at our worst but still loves us just as we are,
who can forgive us even when we can't forgive ourselves,
who believes in our dreams as much as we do –
and encourages us to follow them.

Because we know
we get by with a little help from our friends.

G is for Grace

Grief.
Gratitude.
Grace.
Such important words. Words that are part of our daily lives.

I chose grace for the letter G
because it's part of grief and gratitude
and it's a word we use a lot
but we may have forgotten what it truly means,
because actually
Jesus never mentioned "grace" – his word was love.

Now, my introduction to grace came years ago via my sister's pastor in Atlanta, Georgia,
where she's lived since 1996, so it has a distinctly southern take on it:
"Grace is like grits: you get it whether you order it or not."

Anne Lamott wrote this in her first collection of essays:
"Grace ... is the help you receive when you have no bright ideas left, when you are empty and desperate and have discovered that your best thinking and most charming charm have failed you. Grace is the light or electricity or juice or breeze that takes you from that isolated place and puts you

with others who are as startled and embarrassed and eventually grateful as you are to be there."

Reverend Mark Sandlin, who serves the Presbyterian Church in the United States, says, "Grace is a gift that opens you up towards love and fulfillment. There is no deserving or undeserving it. It just happens. Grace just is."

I like to say that when you've reached the end of your rope, grace ties a knot to help you hold on.

So we're all clear on what grace is, right? Easy peasy.

In early 2020, Canadian pop singer Justin Bieber released a YouTube documentary series called *Seasons*. In one episode, Justin had this to say about the deal he made with God to quit drugs: "I basically said, 'God, if you're real, you get me through this season of stopping these pills and stuff and if you do, I'll do the rest of the work.'"

Bieber admits he got off the drugs but never got around to doing "the rest of the work."

That's the funny – aggravating – great thing about grace:
It doesn't matter if you don't do the work.
It doesn't matter what kind of deal you make,
or whether you hold up your end of the bargain.
Grace is not quid pro quo.
It's not – If you do this, then I'll do that.

That's the human way.
The grace way
is to have love and encouragement
and the possibility of a fresh start
already on offer when you show up.
Grace is always there before you arrive,
always waiting for you to take your seat.

This is why we can't truly wrap our minds around grace –
it's so far beyond what we are capable of.
The selflessness, the lack of ego, the absolute acceptance,
the absence of judgement.
It's radical love: generous, accepting, forgiving.

The true challenge of grace comes with people who are really messing up –
who are messing up so badly even their own family gives up on them –
who just can't seem to stop the downward spiral.
The good news of grace is
love is a gift for them as well.
Just the way they are.
As messy as they are.
Hoping they'll do the work, but nevertheless –
loving them up one side and down the other even when they don't.

And more good news about grace:
while we're judging and gossiping and feeling sorry for those

people trying to do the work,
Jesus
is right there in the midst.
Doing his Jesus thing, which is sitting right there –
in the middle of the mess, in the middle of chaos,
in the middle of the consequences
of another bad decision –
saying, "I'm here. Even if you don't want me here.
I'm not going anywhere.
I'm right here alongside you, no matter what."

Doesn't that make your toes tingle? That kind of love, that kind of devotion –
that kind of kindness?
I'm here, even if you don't want me to be, and I'm not leaving, no matter what you do.

That's the standard we need to aim for. That kind of love.
That kind of graciousness.
That kind of holiness.
Even if it's really, really hard.

Because the hard part of grace is also
the hard part of loving which is also
the hard part of life.

The hard part of life
is a family member with a drug addiction
compounded by mental health issues that are either

the result of the drug use or are exacerbated by drugs.
In the spiral of addiction, this person turns on their family,
turns out on the streets,
fails at court-ordered rehab.
Until the day arrives when the family has to say,
"Enough. We love you, so much, and want you to be well,
but we are at risk here. You can't come by anymore."

We all understand how hard it is
to turn away from a loved one who is suffering,
but who won't accept any help.
It's not a decision one ever wants to have to make,
and it is never made quickly.

How do you reach someone like that?
We are humans and we live in our human world.
We can't control someone else's mind and spirit.
Only they can stop what they are doing.

How does a person turn their life around
through the love of Jesus?
Some guy whose been dead for 2,000 years,
who they likely only heard about in Sunday school
which certainly doesn't give us stories of Jesus loving the drug addict.
How do we reach a person with grace –
with unwavering mercy and acceptance –
if they're locked away in their own torment,
fallen down that deep, dark hole of the consequences of their choices?

How do we reach this person with the love of Jesus
when they make it so hard for us to reach them?

We could take the "extreme grace" route.

There's amazing grace.
There's radical grace – the kind Jesus gives us.
Then there's extreme grace – the kind Jesus really, really
wants *us* to give.

Extreme grace is what we do when things
get really, *really* hard.
We hunker down.
We dig in.
We breathe.
We eat a good breakfast.

We get ready for being extreme.

Being there. Showing up.
With kindness and patience.
With prayer. With hope.
By sitting in silence when there's nothing helpful to say.
Maybe someone sitting there, not saying anything,
just being there,
is the greatest gift of grace.

Because grace is our spirit.

We bring our kind, patient, loving, do-nothing-but-sit-there energy,
and somehow, the person learns they are sitting *with* grace, and *in* grace.
Surrounded by spirit and energy and grace –
cocooned in it, lifted up inside it, carried by it.

Grace is hearing the message, "You are loved and your life has a purpose" over and over –
until we get it. Until we believe it.
Until we wake up, open our eyes, and realize we are loved and we are good enough.

And we are *all* beloved. We are *all* worthy of love, we are *all* worthy of grace.
No matter what. No matter who.

Grace gives us the energy to be present
for as long as it takes
for someone to realize they are capable enough
and strong enough
to do the rest of the work.

It's a tough thing to wrap our minds around
because we like our grudges and our righteous anger,
because there are some hurts and offences
that are unforgivable,
because addictions and obsessions are hard to watch,
let alone understand,

and there are people we simply shouldn't trust;
there are people doing bad things,
and there are just bad people, period.

Here's an idea that caused a tiny explosion in my temporal
lobe, the part of the brain where learning happens:
Because this is Jesus, grace is upside down and radical too.
That means grace is an extravagant gift that benefits not
the giver but the *receiver*.
Yeah, yeah, we know that.

But – *kerplew* goes my lobe – we are *all* receivers.
Shut the front door!
That's the whole point of grace, isn't it? Of Jesus' radical,
redeeming love?
It doesn't benefit the one who gives it –
but rather, the one who *receives* it.

If we help someone –
if we sit with them and listen without judgement,
welcome them into our home when they are a hot mess,
leave a cooler of food on their doorstep when they are
dealing with a crisis –
it's not about how good we are to do those things,
it's about how those things make someone else feel:
Loved. Acknowledged. Welcomed.

And make no mistake: We are all receivers.
All the time. Each day.

As much as we think we are giving love –
and being oh so proud of our selflessness and our thoughtfulness and our niceness –
we are always more *receiver* than giver.

Now,
that was the end of the original message I'd written for church. I finished at four o'clock then went for a walk with the dog.

It was a February afternoon.
There was no wind and big snowflakes were falling straight down. The fields and woods were beautiful and quiet.
It was a good ending
for a day that had started out poorly –
it had started out so badly, in fact, with tears of frustration at nine a.m.,
that I'd told my husband I would get some work done that needed to be done,
and deal with the editors who needed to be dealt with,
then it was going to be an afternoon of
movies and popcorn.
An afternoon to chill out.

I started to work,
and everything got better as the day went on.
A long-awaited writing assignment arrived, as did a "Well done" on a piece I submitted,
and I finished my church message.

As I stood outside in the falling snow, feeling good –
happy, even –
breathing deeply and smiling, even –
I realized:
This is grace.

And that's when the rest of my temporal lobe exploded.
With amazement. With amazing grace!

Here I was, receiving an unexpected gift.
Now, at the end of the day,
I could see the grace-filled moments
upon which this moment in the falling snow was built.

Oh, I'd done the work. I have faith in my skills,
I love writing and it went well, so of course I felt better at the end of the day.
I'd accomplished a lot and was pleased with my work.
Even better, someone else was pleased with my work.

But I needed grace – love and mercy and holy energy –
to get me through my doubts, my frustrations,
my complaining, my lack of faith.
I needed grace to dry my tears and get my butt upstairs to my office *to do the work*.
I needed grace to get me standing outside in the falling snow, being grateful.

And that's the most important thing to know about grace:
It's all about the gratitude you feel
for everything you receive.
When you are cracked open and filled with
peace and possibility,
when you have relaxed your grip on that knot and have
pulled yourself back up the rope,
when you are humbled by the beauty of the world
and reminded you are not alone and you are loved,
when you see the snowflakes resting lightly
on your dog's nose,
you can't help but be thankful.

H IS FOR House

God is in the slums, in the cardboard boxes where the poor play house. God is in the silence of a mother who has infected her child with a virus that will end both their lives. God is in the cries heard under the rubble of war. God is in the debris of wasted opportunity and lives, and God is with us if we are with them.
— BONO, LEADER SINGER OF U2

Early in 2020, my then-16-year-old niece Mimi painted seven slabs of wood each a different colour of the rainbow, then painted the following words on them:
>In this house
>We believe
>Science is real
>Women's rights are human rights
>Kindness is everything
>Love is love
>Black lives matter

Her father nailed the boards to a tree in the front yard of their home in Atlanta, Georgia
(much to the delight of their Republican neighbours with Vote Trump signs stuck in their lawns).

This inspired me to create the same signs for my yard in Nova Scotia.

After all the work, I couldn't bring myself to nail each brightly coloured board to one of our trees and leave them outside during a Canadian winter, so I took my painting easel to church and stacked the signs one on top of the other on the easel at the front of the church. They made a nice backdrop for our online worship.

Stained glass windows. Large felt banners. Slabs of wood painted in rainbow colours.
It all belongs in church.
In God's house.

In this house,
we believe.

That's how the United Church of Canada's creed begins: "We believe in God, who has created and is creating, who has come in Jesus, the Word made flesh, to reconcile and make new, who works in us and others by the Spirit."

To reconcile and make new.
Reconcile – to bring us together, to unify, with love.
Make new – to think and act differently – in a new way, with a new truth,
so that we may have new life.

Life that includes and respects and loves everyone.

Everyone ... because God works in us *and in others.*

Others.
As in everyone.

Everyone who dwells in the house of God is blessed.

In this house,
there are many dwelling places.

Another way of saying this is God's house is big. Huge.
It's a great, big, huge tent that can be set up anywhere.
Everyone can fit into the tent.
Everyone is welcome inside the tent.
EVERYONE.
Us and others.

In God's house are many rooms.
Lots of space for lots of people.
Because there are many kinds of people.
A mosaic of people – of colours and abilities,

And Jesus loves them all.
Jesus welcomes them all.
When Jesus is "swinging the door,"
no one gets it closed in their face.

When Jesus is working the front desk, there is always a room available – and totally accessible – for each person.

You see, Jesus saw his work as a fulfillment of the law.
The Mosaic law, the laws and the prophets, were the path leading to Jesus.
Once Jesus introduced people to his new ideas for living in community, the Mosaic law,
what we know as "the Ten Commandments,"
was no longer relevant.
Not because it didn't matter
but because of these new ideas of Jesus.
(Oh, how we love someone coming along with new ideas.)

Jesus walked and talked and hung out with the weak and the poor, those working long hours and those who couldn't get a job, those who couldn't take care of themselves,
in order to show everyone what this new law looked like.
Because it was a new way, a new truth, a new life.

New, new, new. Not the old. The old was done.
Fulfilled.
Obsolete.
Jesus gave us
the new commandments:
Love God and love your neighbour.
AND, as he said in the hours just before his death:
Love one another as I have loved you.

Love one another. A command –
a verb –
not a feeling but a doing –
go and love.

Love each other and love others as I have loved you.

And what kind of love did Jesus bring to the table that sits in this house?
A kind and merciful love for everyone.
A unifying and all-encompassing love that looks at each one of us –

in our self-centredness,
in our defensiveness,
in our judgy-ness and gossiping,
in our worry and our overthinking,

as we cross to the other side of the road to avoid speaking to someone,
as we complain about people getting free money from the government,
as we pop too many pills, drink too many glasses of wine, get a new tattoo,

when our anxiety overwhelms us or our depression drags us into the dark hole,
when the trauma of our childhood makes us fearful and hypercritical as adults –

a unifying and all-encompassing love that looks at each one of us,

sees a hot mess,
and still says,
"Come with me. Come as you are, just as you are."

Sit.
Breathe.
Cry.
Rest.

Then after a while, once we've calmed down and got ourselves a bit more together,
changed our clothes and had a cup of tea,
once we've experienced the grace of do-overs and fresh starts,
Jesus says,
"Now go, and love others as I have loved you."

In this house.
In God's house.
In the house Jesus calls us to build and keep building.
To create and keep creating.

Because we believe.
In love.
In loving each other as Jesus loved us.

So,
if you look at the phrases on these signs and recoil,
if you look at any one of these signs and say, "But ..."
consider a second set of signs I painted later, using words
and phrases right from the Bible:
> In this house
> We believe
> in peace, love and unity
> in loving our neighbours
> and our enemies
> in kindness, mercy and justice
> in walking humbly with our God

and ask yourself what it means when Jesus says,
"Love one another as I have loved you"?

It wasn't a "do as I say" command –
it was a "do as I do" command.
Love God.
Love each other.
And do it all as I did it.

Because in this house,
we believe in Jesus.

And we believe
the world needs more Jesus.

I IS FOR Image of God

*No one is born hating another person because of
the colour of his skin, or his background, or his religion.
People must learn to hate, and if they can learn to hate,
they can be taught to love.*
— NELSON MANDELA

When I speak about love and acceptance and kindness
and mercy and taking care of each other,
I feel confident and passionate.
The ground beneath my feet feels solid, supporting my
convictions, my beliefs, my faith.

My trust in my heart and my instincts.

When I wrote a sermon about the phrase
"created in the image of God,"
with texts spread all around me – the thoughts of other
Christian writers, information from biblical scholars, online
articles by experts –
I could feel the confidence and passion leaking out of me.

When I was finished writing that sermon, the ground beneath my feet felt unstable –
I had too much information from too many sources and it
wasn't coming together concisely,

the sermon felt overwhelmed with information
and a kind of "then there's this" and "there's also this" back
and forth.

My head was spinning.

But I didn't want to abandon this choice for the letter I –
because the phrase "created in the image of God"
has been on my radar, like an unidentified flying object,
for a number of years.
It's a phrase I come across often –
people toss it out there because it sounds really cool, really
holy – and
it's something we're supposed to say –
but do we ever stop think what it really means?

As Inigo Montoya says to Vizzini in the 1987 movie *The Princess Bride*,
"You keep using that word. I do not think it means what you think it means."

The more we use the phrase "created in the image of God,"
the less we "get" it.
But like grace, it's important to understand the words of our faith,
the words and phrases and ideas we think are cool,
and to dive deep into their meanings, even if we're wary of what we might learn.

As I sat at my desk, I had a choice to make between my confidence and passion,
and my research and the experts.

You know what I decided?
To do what we are always told to do – Be true to yourself.
I decided to believe in myself, in my skills, in my brain.
To trust in my heart and my instincts.

Sarah Bessey, a Canadian Christian writer, said,
"Sometimes relaxing our grip is the most holy work we can do, you know?"

And that's what works for me:
letting go and breathing out,
walking the dog, having a bath, washing dishes, doing yoga,
finding stillness and listening,
then following the voice,
the spirit,
the energy.

It took me a long time to figure it out, but this is how I operate as a spiritual being
who happens to think and write: I sit down, place my fingers on the keyboard.
And I relax.
I let whatever is in my mind drop down into my heart,
and then through my arms and out my fingertips comes what I really believe –

from my instincts, from my heart, from my spirit —
about a topic.

Unless the topic is the one about how we're created in the image of God.
In the last few years, I avoided the phrase,
avoided my questions and doubts,
avoided asking anyone what it means.

Until now. Now I really needed that instinctive creative process to work its magic.
Because I don't think "the image of God" means what we think it means.

The phrase "the image of God" comes from the first book of the Bible, Genesis, and the story about the creation of our world. The language around God is male-centred: "Then God said, 'Let us make humankind in our image, according to our likeness …'"
Then: "So God created humankind in his image, in the image of God he created them, male and female he created them."

In the second chapter of Genesis, we get a more detailed account of human creation involving dust and breath, and eventually a rib: "God formed man from the dust of the ground, and breathed into his nostrils the breath of life."
Later: "God took one of the man's ribs … and made it into a woman."

We could argue that the way this creation happens – God making humans – we could think the "image" refers to "looks" and "appearance."

Thankfully, my annotated Bible provides this explanation for these verses:
"Image and likeness are often interpreted to be a spiritual likeness between God and humanity."

A spiritual likeness. So not looks and appearance at all.
We are not created in the image of God –
we are created by the *energy* of God,
and infused with the spirit of God
so that we become a spiritual likeness with God.

So what about the Genesis story?
In her book *Inspired*, about learning to love the Bible again, author Rachel Held Evans wrote,
"Contrary to what many of us are told, Israel's origin stories weren't designed to answer scientific, twenty-first century questions about the beginning of the universe or the biological evolution of human beings, but rather were meant to answer then-pressing ancient questions about the nature of God and God's relationship to humans."

It's *not* a literal story.
And taking it literally nullifies everything that is beautiful and mystical and mysterious and sacred – and infinite and universal.

Taking it literally takes the spiritual out of it.
Erases our connection to the spiritual likeness of God.
To breathing and becoming and being an act of love.

If the story isn't literal, then it's symbolic. It's a metaphor.
A metaphor, and a very beautiful one –
a metaphor portraying our *relationship* with God.

The creation story that comes to us
from the ancient peoples
is about the nature of God,
and about God's relationship with humankind.

It's about our *spiritual* likeness, not a *physical* likeness.

We are formed by energy –
and we all contain a common energy.
Call that God, call it divine,
call it the universe, call it cosmic energy,
call it the result of the Big Bang –
it is what makes us human, and it makes us connected.

Some of us would call that "the image of God" but we
could just as easily call it
the breath of God
the spirit of God
the spark of God
or even the nature of God.

It's the same as when we talk about seeing the face of God when we look at each other.
Or when we look in the mirror.
Our reflection isn't meant to show us an actual image of God – a physical representation.
We are who God *is*,
not what God looks like.
Infused with God's energy, we are to be *like* God –
not in the way we look but in the way we act.

And that, for Christians, is where Jesus comes in.

Now ... from the ancient origin story in Genesis, which is not meant to be a scientific explanation of how we came to be, but a cultural explanation for a specific people,
we get another I-word related to the image of God:
Incarnation.

Also not meant to be a scientific explanation.

Gospel writers Matthew and Mark say that Jesus is going to establish God's reign on earth –
not through war or conquest,
but through love and sacrifice.

Gospel writer John gives us "the image of God" as
"God became flesh and dwelt among us."
The spiritual likeness becoming a physical likeness.

Jesus is the image of God –
the spiritual likeness –
the soul and the heart of God –
and his gospel is the new story about the nature of God,
and God's relationship with humankind and creation.

As Sarah Bessey wrote in her memoir called *Miracles and Other Reasonable Things*, "Even if we have strayed from the original blessing of our made-in-the-image-of-God selves, we are blessed again, redeemed, because of the incarnation of Jesus Christ, all of humanity blessed because he broke through and embodied humanity, showing us how to be truly human, all over again."

Truly human.
In the spiritual likeness of God – a God of love.
In the human likeness of Jesus.

So that we become humans who are compassionate and merciful, humble and just.
Humans who know they are loved and their life has purpose – to love others.

At this point, my brain melts. And that's okay.
I'm very glad I tackled this concept, glad I discovered that yes, it's big and it's deep
but it's really wonderful.
And it's actually understandable.
And we don't need to know what God looks like!

Remember? "I am what I am."
So,
God can be clouds
and an old dog lying in the sun
and red-ripe cherry tomatoes hanging heavy on the vine.
God can be your grandmother
and that mama bear with three cubs
and the waves pounding the shore during a Nor'easter.

I am
is clouds
and dogs and vegetables,
grandmothers and aunties,
bears and deer and moles,
waves and seaweed and sand.

I am
is love and hope
joy and peace
mercy and kindness
hospitality and tolerance
forgiveness and welcome
humility and empathy
acceptance and understanding.
Also: sarcasm, irony and wit,
laughter, and tears, and eye rolls.

From a small, limited, literal image of God,
suddenly God is everything

and everywhere.
Including that face reflected in the mirror.

Ideas like this,
these kinds of questions and explorations,
aren't meant to undermine our faith and our beliefs.
They are meant to *deepen* them.
The more we understand our faith, God and Jesus,
the more we understand ourselves
and the purpose of our life.
Not just our personal life, but our life as a people.
As a community of faith, as a community of humans.

The more open and accepting we are of new information,
and of listening to our own hearts,
and the less literal we are about our Bible and our beliefs,
the more comfortable we will be
with different images of God,
with all the images of God.

The more we understand about
our universal and timeless stories,
told over and over
since we began sitting around a campfire
asking questions about why we are here,
the more comfortable we will be
with seeing the image of God –

the spiritual likeness of God –
in every face we meet.

The more comfortable we will become with our God-infused humanity.

As 15th-century German-Dutch canon Thomas à Kempis said,
"To say that I am made in the image of God is to say that love is the reason for my existence, for God is love."

So we are love:
created by the energy of love
and infused with the spirit of love.

Now, if I may be so bold,
I'm going to rewrite those verses in Genesis:

"God said to Spirit,
'Let's make humankind in our imagination,
according to what we like … so God created humankind with imagination,
God created male and female …
and gay and lesbian,
and trans and non-binary,
and black and white,
and brown,

and pink,
and short and tall,
and thin and sturdy and well-padded,
young and old and middle-aged,
and God blessed them.

And it was good.

J is for Justice

*I would like to be known as a person who
is concerned about freedom and equality and
justice and prosperity for all people.*
— ROSA PARKS

We normally think of justice as
"punishment for the wrongdoer" –
underlined with plenty of righteousness and judgement
and holier-than-them.

But let's consider justice in the context of our faith.
Justice is a way of "being right in the world" –
this doesn't mean "I'm right and you're wrong" but rather,
to be in right relationship.
It means to live – to act and think and speak – in the way
God wants us to live.

Just let that sink in for a moment –
because it's the difference between being in the world –
but not of it.

Justice means to live – to think and speak and act –
in the way God wants us to.
The way Jesus wants us to.
To be kind and merciful and humble.

Which, according to the origins of our faith, is the Hebrew concept of *shalom*.

Shalom is one of those words that lost the richness of its meaning through simplification.
Many of us may think *shalom* is used simply as a greeting or a blessing –
Peace be with you –
but originally, it encompassed God's vision for us.
Not merely peace, and an absence of conflict,
but complete harmony,
between God and humankind, between human and human, and between human and nature.

Shalom is all the blessings of peace, harmony, wholeness, prosperity, well-being, and tranquility.

Can I get an amen for *shalom*?

Justice is defined as "fair treatment" and that's the foundation of "right relationship":
peace, harmony, wholeness, prosperity, well-being, and tranquility –
for everyone.

That's the vision of *shalom* we get throughout the Hebrew scriptures:
Seek justice.
Bring forth justice.

Establish justice.
Act with justice.
Do justice.

As a young Jewish boy,
this is what Jesus learned at synagogue.
He would have known all about *shalom*.
Long before he started his ministry as an adult,
he was listening and learning about justice
from the prophets.

And from the "Song of Hannah," from 1 Samuel 2, which doesn't use the word "justice" in it, but *does* include verses like these:
"The bows of the mighty are broken, but the feeble gird on strength. Those who were full have hired themselves out for bread, but those who were hungry are fat with spoil … [The Lord] raises up the poor from the dust; he lifts the needy from the ash heap, to make them sit with princes …" (4–5, 8A, NRSV).

Sound familiar?
"He has brought down the powerful from their thrones but has lifted up the lowly;
he has filled the hungry with good things but has sent the rich away empty" (LUKE 1:52–53, NRSV).

That's a verse from another song, Mary's "Magnificat," recorded in the gospel of Luke.

We usually hear it on the first Sunday of Advent.

So *shalom* – justice and fair treatment –
is the early influence of Jesus –
it's what he heard throughout his childhood and his studies at the temple.
Shalom is the reason he grew up to believe he had to try to free Israel,
and the people of God,
from the oppression and occupation of the Romans.
To bring about peace, harmony, wholeness, prosperity, well-being, and tranquility
through the new way he envisioned.
Peace through love, not violence –
through arms that reach out to help, not arms that kill.

What an example he sets for the 21st century,
when it seems we are held captive
by the same kind of empire,
one that is just as oppressive, violent, and greedy,
just as hierarchical, patriarchal, and racist,
just as deeply rooted and resistant to change.

We tend to focus on how Jesus' ministry ends: with his trial and death –
after all, his crucifixion and resurrection are two of the pillars of our Christian faith –
but we can't underestimate the load-bearing beam that is his ministry,
especially when it comes to justice.

The gospel of Luke also gives us the beginning of Jesus' ministry when he stands up in the synagogue in his hometown of Nazareth and unrolls a scroll to quote the prophet Isaiah:
"The Spirit of the Lord is upon me,
because he has anointed me to bring good news to
the poor.
He has sent me to proclaim release to the captives and
recovery of sight to the blind,
to let the oppressed go free" (LUKE 4:18, NRSV).

Holy Hannah!
This moment is Jesus clearly stating the work he has come to do.

The work of justice.

Bringing good news to the poor.
Releasing those who are captive.
Giving sight to those who cannot see.
Freeing the oppressed.

The work of justice.
For everyone.

Jesus didn't come to save people from hell, or to give them a ticket out of this world.
His purpose was to redeem humanity from itself –
from conflict and despair, violence and oppression,

from ignorance and resistance, defensiveness and fear,
from greed and materialism –
and create a lasting peace –
in this world.
In their lifetime.

Raised on *shalom*,
Jesus made it his life's work, his mission.

The Kin-dom of God is *shalom*.

Scottish/Australian writer and retired minister Moira Laidlaw says,
"The prophet Isaiah proclaimed – and Jesus embodied – God's call to reach out and care for those who are brokenhearted and those who mourn, people who are abused and oppressed, who are powerless to make changes for good in their lives."

We can't call ourselves followers of Jesus, or people of the Christian faith, if we don't do all of that – if we aren't seeking, establishing, bringing forth, acting with and doing justice.
Like Jesus, we've all grown up hearing this stuff.
Why is it such a struggle for us to embody it too?

Nancy Mairs, an American Catholic author and essayist, put it brilliantly:

"That's what we're here for: to make the world new. We know what to do: seek justice, love mercy, walk humbly, treat every person as though she were yourself. These are not complicated instructions. It's much harder to decipher the instructions for putting together a tricycle than it is to understand these."

There's a verse in the gospel of Matthew that doesn't use the word "justice" but epitomizes the core of Jesus' ethical teachings:
"In everything, do to others as you would have them do to you" (MATTHEW 7:12).

Our whole faith is supposed to be based on *shalom* –
on justice –
on treating others the way we want to be treated,
and yet: We aren't behaving any better, or differently, in the 21st century
than people seemed to be behaving in the first and second centuries.

So how does the work of *shalom* become part of our work?

We are called to "do justice" –
but what if we also are called to "undo injustice"?

Seeking, establishing, bringing forth, acting with,
and doing justice

must also involve the undoing of injustice.
Righting wrongs.
Applying what we've learned from past experiences.

Doing justice is more than demanding it.
It's even more than helping.
That's good work but it merely deals with the symptoms.
Undoing injustice requires us to move beyond feeding the poor and clothing the naked,
making donations to the food bank and knitting socks for those who sleep on the streets.

According to Kathy Evans, an associate professor of education at Eastern Mennonite University, justice is about "recognizing that members of certain groups are disproportionately vulnerable to injustices – who experience violence, including death, conflict, disrespect and discrimination for no other reason than their gender or race, skin colour or disability."

She says we must recognize that "in order to do justice, we must undo the injustices."

Begin by:
Seeking
Bringing forth
Establishing
Acting with

not only
justice
but also
kindness
mercy
and humility.

In order to start our work for a free and fair world where oppression and inequality no longer exist, we, too, need to stand in our "synagogue" – whatever our holy space is – and announce,
"This is the work I've come to do."

K IS FOR Kingdom

Your task is not to seek for love, but merely seek and find all the barriers within yourself that you have built against it.
— RUMI

There is a discussion ongoing about the term "kingdom" which has to do with translations and meanings. Synonyms could include "empire" or "dominion," or even "reign."
It also has to do with the concept of "king" – a male ruler – and the clear link with conquest and colonialism.
Now, in the 21st century, I find myself balking at the term "kingdom" as archaic and irrelevant.
The replacement is kin-dom,
suggesting the idea we are all kin.

I'm sticking with the word kingdom here, however, because it is the familiar term we have from Jesus' teachings. Those listening to Jesus would have known exactly what he meant: He was railing against the kingdom of Herod, within the Roman Empire –
and promoting a better kingdom, the kingdom of God.

What does the kingdom of God look like?

The kingdom of God is not a physical place. It's neither heaven nor the church.
It's Jesus, and it's us. It's among us and within us.

We enter or create or *become* the kingdom of God by living in right relationship with God.
It's about shalom –
the blessings of peace, harmony, wholeness, prosperity, well-being, and tranquility –
and about the Beatitudes –
the blessings for the despairing, the grieving, the humble, the activists, the caregivers, the humanitarians, the collaborators, the holy troublemakers, and the victims.

And we need to remember the whole point of Jesus' life and ministry.
For all he talks about the kingdom of God, Jesus takes what we *think* a kingdom is –
and turns it upside down.
Because with Jesus, the kingdom of God does not look like we expect, or want, it to look like.

As Jesus teaches, God's blessings are for the poor, the merciful, the hungry, and the humble. Or as Fred Rogers – of the Neighbourhood – said, "The kingdom of God is for the broken-hearted."

Basically, it doesn't matter how much money we have, or how much food we eat, or how nice our car and house is,

how much stuff we have –
– if we aren't living by the laws of justice, mercy,
and kindness …
well, we're not building, or even getting near, the kingdom
(or the kin-dom, for that matter).

The kingdom, or kin-dom, of God was the message and
mission of Jesus.
He proclaimed it, he taught it, and he lived it.
He walked the talk – that the kingdom is here.
It was the reason he would die on a cross,
rather than sit on a throne:
to bring about the kingdom of God for all humanity.
For all who believed in him and followed his way.

This is where the focus and faith of the church needs to be.
Creating the kingdom of God. Here. Now. At all times.
This is the work of the church –
"The work I've come to do," as Jesus said at the start of his
ministry.

Jesus said, "The kingdom of God is among you."
At the time, those in the crowd who questioned him were
thinking of a kingdom that would bring material and political benefits, but in saying that Jesus shifted the emphasis from future expectations to the actual presence of the
kingdom in his ministry.

On earth as it is in heaven.
Among you, right here, right now.

Watch the news and read the newspapers and you'll think we have a long way to go
in creating the kingdom of God on earth as it is in heaven.
It's the 21st century and we're still reminding people that the kingdom of God
is meant to happen here on earth.
It feels like an endless, uphill struggle, that it's one step forward and two steps back.
It feels like it will never truly happen.
It certainly appears that way.

But we're wrong.
The kingdom of God already exists on earth –
it's already an *actual presence.*
We just need to see with new eyes because if you watch the news and read the newspapers –
you will see the kingdom of God is here.

That is our hope and our encouragement – that the kingdom of God truly is among us.

So I'll ask again: What does the kingdom of God look like?

It looks like people taking care of each other.
It looks like people linking arms with each other.

It looks like people treating neighbours
as extended family.
It looks like a close-knit, functioning body
where each member is affected by what happens to the other members.

It looks like what we heard about justice, and hearing what Jesus considered the work he'd come to do:
    feeding the hungry
    clothing the naked
    blessing the poor
    giving sight to the blind
    caring for the sick and infirm

According to author Herb Montgomery, the director of Renewed Hearts Ministry, a faith and social justice non-profit organization based in West Virginia, Jesus showed people a new way to achieve the kingdom:
"When Jesus says, 'the Kingdom is not coming with signs to be observed,' he is rejecting the specific way in which prophets had led masses of Jewish people to their deaths at the hands of Roman soldiers. Jesus instead offered a new vision for human society in the form of a *community* that practiced nonviolent resistance, liberation, and reparation, with the hope of both personal and societal *transformation*. This kingdom was within their grasp."

The kingdom as "kommunity."

So what does the community of God look like?

Well, let me repeat:
It looks like people taking care of each other.
It looks like people linking arms with each other.
It looks like people treating neighbours
as extended family.
It looks like a close-knit, functioning body
where each member is affected by
what happens to the other members.

It looks like stories in the news and on social media.

It looks like a guy named Shea Serrano, who, in the early days of the pandemic lockdown in the United States, went onto his Twitter account and tweeted, "Who needs help?"
That's it. Three words: "Who needs help?"
Serrano – and others who joined him – paid phone bills, medication, a student loan payment, a monthly insurance payment, a car payment.
He gave money to a woman expecting her first baby just because she was worried.

No questions asked. No judgement rendered.
Just three more words: "We got you."

That's what the community of God looks like.

Graphic artist Lori Hetteen wrote, "I can't rid myself of the notion that we carry each other. So much of the way God talks to and about us is communal. We're a people. A collective. I do well when you do well. When I see your good, I am seeking my own."

Jesus' vision for living was communal,
rather than individualistic.
Each one of us, with all our needs and wants, exists in the context of a larger community –
whether we like it or not.
Jesus' vision is meant to address injustice, oppression, marginalization, and violence,
to ensure that those who are last get their bills paid first.

When you consider that those first-century issues are still faced in the 21st century,
it's no wonder the world needs more Jesus.

The kingdom of God is the community of God.

Just changing that word brings it right down to earth.
Right down to our space.
Right down to our yards and our tables, our churches and our pews.
In community – with God, with Jesus, and with each other.

How does the idea that the kingdom of God is actually a community,

our community, us living in community, make us feel?
Scared or inspired?
Defensive or empowered?
Apprehensive or brave?

In March 2020, just after we locked down in Canada and the United States, Ann Dunn, a writer and editor living Brooklyn, New York, wrote the following in a post on her Instagram account – but I think it's worth lifting up for our post-pandemic world: "Make more communities. Expand your ability to care whatever that may mean for you. Learn about harm reduction and compassion and commit to it as a path for peace.
There's no other way forward.
There is only what is crashing behind us. Not me. US."

Community.
Compassion.
Peace.
Us.

The community of God exists – and it's here, now.
Let's not miss it,
even as it's manifesting itself in front of us.
Let's not be deliberately blind to it – and to our part in it.
We are called to create it, but also maintain it.
To build it and rebuild it.
To re-create it.

To take those upside-down, radical blessings of Jesus, and LIVE them.
To embody them like he did.

The kingdom of God is for the brave-hearted.

L IS FOR Liminal Space

*All great spirituality is what we do with our pain.
If we do not transform our pain, we will
transmit it to those around us.*
~ RICHARD ROHR

Poet William Blake wrote, "In the universe, there are things that are known and things that are unknown, and in between, there are doors."

Most of us are familiar with the old adage, "When one door closes, another one opens."

Whether a new one opens right away or not, those doors are each a threshold.
When we stand on a threshold, waiting and wondering – we are in a liminal space.

The word liminal comes from the Latin word, *limens*, meaning threshold.
Also – edge and doorway.

A space between then and now.

What we experienced during the pandemic –
waves one, two and three, and four,

with circuit breaker lockdowns
and slow vaccination rollouts,
with those slow to get vaccinated –
that was the waiting period
between the Time Before and the Time After.

A time of waiting, and wondering;
a time of enduring;
a time of just being –
standing at the threshold of what was,
without knowing what will come
when we step through that door.

That is liminal space: A transition from one way of living and being, to a new one.

Such as the other "virus" revealed in 2020: racism.
I'd argue this is an even greater liminal space in which many of us are "doing the work" to make changes to the system, understanding that we are standing on a more significant threshold –
and hoping we don't fall back through the door we're trying to close behind us.

Richard Rohr, a Franciscan priest, calls liminal space "that graced time when we are not certain or in control, when something genuinely new can happen."

What liminal spaces do we experience in our personal lives?

The time between a test and the results.
The time around a person's dying –
their coming in and going out.
The period of intense grief after the loss of
a loved one or a relationship,
a pet,
a job, an identity, a dream.

Betrayal can create a liminal space –
that time between what happened and moving on,
and the liminal space of waiting to forgive or be forgiven.

It is often a period of discomfort,
of uncertainty and confusion,
of outright fear.
A space, an experience to resist, to avoid.

It's not always a negative thing, or a loss, however.

Since we have a word for it, since it can be described as the space between
"no longer" and "not yet" – with all the hope and potential of "not yet,"
we can view liminal space as the necessary place
that is a welcome pit stop
on our human journey.

Liminal space
can be a time we take away from our regular lives
to pause, breathe, and live in the moment.
It can be a time when we take a long look at our faith, at our doubts, at our fears –
when we ask questions, come to new conclusions or re-commit to our beliefs.
It can be a time when we get curious about our potential and re-imagine dreams.

We can make a leap of faith from a liminal space.

Whether it is welcome or dreaded,
liminal space is about transformation.

In terms of our faith, a scary and uncertain time is meant to be about experiencing it,
not merely surviving it but thriving because of it.
It's about using "isolation" – whether down time or retreat or quarantine – as a chance to explore who we are and what we are called to do.
It's about standing in front of a door, on the threshold, and recognizing we are being called to change.

How do we find spirit and grace – courage and strength – in liminal space?

Our foundation is believing that we are not alone,
that God is with us,

that liminal space is a safe space where we are loved and accepted and forgiven,
empowered and inspired *no matter what.*
Our foundation is believing
the ultimate purpose of liminal space is
to keep us in, or bring us back to, right relationship with God, and with ourselves.

Liminal space can provide an opening to learn something new and to discover something –
a gift
we didn't know we possessed,
or aren't sure we want to accept.

When the pandemic lockdown first began in late March 2020, I struggled with the "gift"
of leadership,
of stepping deeper into a role I'd resisted all my life.
It took the transformation of how we offered worship and maintained connection to make me see how my call to serve as a lay worship leader extends into the greater community.

Funny how what I considered my dis-comfort zone – the pulpit and the sanctuary – became my comfort zone as I offered worship and spiritual connection in new and different ways.

When the pandemic lockdown first began, retired American Episcopal bishop and academic Steven Charleston shared his thoughts on Facebook, and here are some of them:

"We are not afraid of this crisis for we have been made ready for it.
We have devoted our lives to the belief that something greater than fear or disease guides human history.
We have studied, prayed, and grown in the Spirit.
Now we come to the call to use what we believe …
We are the calm in the midst of a storm.
Stand your ground and let your light shine so others may see it and find their faith as well."

These are words worth considering deeply
in terms of our faith,
as followers of Jesus, for a world that needs more Jesus,
as we move forward into our new world
and – hopefully – apply the lessons we learned and the insights we gained.

Which, as always, come back to:
We are called to love our neighbours –
to take care of each other.
To protect and free and lift up friends and employees and strangers.

The liminal space we experienced through the global pandemic reminds us
that in any threshold situation,
it is best to let go of our expectations of when a period of tribulation will end,
to let go of judging it as "unwelcome,"
to let go of resistance and denial.

Instead, we can see whatever liminal space we inhabit –
by choice or by chance –
as a sign that genuine change, on a personal level, on a community level and on a global level,
is possible.

We can start to experience
peace in the confusion,
joy in the discomfort, and
clarity in the uncertainty.

Just as Jesus did in the last few hours of his life.

After supper with his disciples but before Judas arrives with the authorities,
Jesus enters into a liminal space –
where he prays for himself and for his disciples,
for his life's purpose to be fulfilled –
in the time between his final gathering with his friends and followers,
and his trial and crucifixion.

Imagine how he felt,
suspended in that moment between life and death,
between his life's work and his life's purpose,
between the courage to pursue his ministry
and the courage to pursue the fulfillment of his mission.

What a time and what a prayer:

"I'm saying these things in the world's hearing
So my people can experience
My joy completed in them.
I gave them your word;
The godless world hated them because of it,
Because they didn't join the world's ways,
Just as I didn't join the world's ways.

I have made your very being known to them –
Who you are and what you do –
And continue to make it known,
So that your love for me
Might be in them
Exactly as I am in them" (JOHN 17:13–16, 25–26, MSG).

The disciples themselves entered into a liminal space
after Jesus' death –
a space between what was and what was not yet.
Then Jesus revealed himself to them,
appeared to the disciples –
a new door opened.

The gate.
The way.
The truth: I am the way forward.
Step through this doorway into a new life.

The husband of a friend of mine died in the month of September and she decided to spend the winter in another province with her son and grandchildren.

How appropriate the season of winter,
when everything is quiet, shut down, frozen,
was her liminal time.
Her period of waiting
between the life she once knew but could no longer live,
and the new life she would create for herself when she returned home.
One door closed, another had yet to open,
and my friend waited on the threshold,
grieving, mourning, taking comfort from family,
gathering strength and wisdom
for her new journey.

Whenever we find ourselves in a liminal space –
a time set apart, a suspension bridge
between then and now –
we need to recognize it as a point or place of
entering or beginning.
Where we stand – on the threshold – is the way forward.

We are being offered a gift – of time, of stillness,
of contemplation.
We are being offered a gift – of reconnecting with God
in a deeper way than we ever dared.
We are being offered a gift – of becoming more true,
God-breathed, Spirit-inspired,
Jesus-empowered selves than ever before.

M is for Miracle

Miracles happen every day. Change your perception of what a miracle is, and you'll see them all around you.
— JON BON JOVI

There are two ways of looking at a miracle:
the big, fancy, awe-inspiring, mind-blowing,
did-you-see-that? miracle
we often associate with
curing someone of illness or disease.
The "woo hoo!" miracle.
The "everything is all right now" miracle.
The "God is good" miracle.

Then there is the ordinary, everyday, quiet, unassuming,
no-one-is-really-paying-attention miracle.
The "suffering happens" miracle.
The "good grief" miracle.
The "God is in the darkness" miracle.
Otherwise known as: Life.

The life we wake up to every day.
The eye-opening life,
in whatever way that happens for each of us.
The miraculous life we get to live every day,
even if it hurts,

even if it challenges,
even if it seems impossible.
The kind of life where there is
darkness *and* light,
sorrow *and* joy,
laughter *and* tears,
sickness *and* health,
dying *and* living.

The simple miracle that life isn't either/or – it's *and*.

Wendell Berry, a beloved American writer, farmer, and environmentalist, suggests we overlook many of the miracles around us: "Whoever really has considered the lilies of the field or the birds of the air and pondered the improbability of their existence in this warm world within the cold and empty stellar distances will hardly balk at the turning of water into wine – which was, after all, a very small miracle. We forget the greater and still continuing miracle by which water (with soil and sunlight) is turned into grapes."

Anyone else exhale on a long, hard "Of course!" when they read that?

Ordinary, everyday miracles.
The miracles of living, breathing, creating, growing, expanding, contracting,
impregnating, pollinating, dying, birthing,
that take place every day on every inch of this earth.

The ordinary, everyday miracles that we take for granted.

Everything around us is a miracle.
Our existence.
All creation.
The resources that provide for us.
Each other.

That bumblebees are able to fly.

Ordinary, everyday miracles.
The kind that nourish us, sustain us, uplift us, renew us.

And motivate us.
Seriously, if that large body can be lifted up and moved around by wings so small ...
(Bumblebees are one of the few known pollinators of potatoes so one could argue bumblebees perform the miracle of giving us french fries.)

There are some pretty other amazing miracles out there.

Some writers riff about quantum physics
and the miracle of particles and atoms and molecules.

Some writers riff about sex and the miracle of creating a life in what is an extraordinarily complicated process.

Those are really mind-blowing miracles with a whole lot of details.

So allow me to be rather simple and ordinary
and riff about how amazing our senses are.

I see you, you see me.
We see eagles and the river and the smiles of children.
I hear you, you hear me.
We hear music and dogs barking and laughter.
We *feel* music and dogs barking and laughter.
We hug – and we can feel our hearts beating.
We hug – and *hear* our hearts beating.
We can smell bread baking and spring coming.
We can smell if it's going to snow or rain.
We can taste wine and bread, cookies and tea,
the salt on our skin.
We can feel the sun on our skin and the prickle of a beard on our cheek.

The fact we get to experience all or some or even one of those things is a miracle.
A moment to be grateful for.
The ordinary, everyday miracles of life.

Life. Living.
Which means being in relationship with each other.
We are alive – and we are not alone.

Because of those particles and atoms and molecules,
because of sex and sperm and eggs and surviving that whole process,
we are all connected.
By life. By living.

And by death.

Wait – what?
Death is a miracle?

When we talk about death as a metaphor –
in the context of the *meaning* of Jesus' life and death,
and his teachings,
then yes, death is a miracle.

Let's consider the story of Jesus raising Lazarus from death:
Jesus invites Lazarus to new life.
Jesus doesn't go into the tomb and drag Lazarus out.
He stands outside the tomb and asks Lazarus to come out on his own.
Lazarus has to choose.

And this is where we are in our humanity:
Do we choose death –
as in, do we choose to be selfish, greedy, power-hungry –
to be self-centred, covetous, arrogant?

OR

When offered the opportunity to come out of the shadows, to be saved, to be resurrected,
do we choose life –
as in, do we choose to be considerate and caring and concerned, to be selfless and fearless and brave –
to make decisions based on how they will shelter those who are weaker, more vulnerable, more at risk?
Do we choose to be the humans God intended us to be –
asks us to be –
desperately wants us to be: a people who act out of love rather than indifference,
who help rather than hate,
who are willing to sacrifice their way of living for the well-being of others?

Do we choose to step out into
the abundant life offered by Jesus,
a life of compassion, mercy, and humility
when we have everything we need?
OR
Do we choose to remain surrounded by what is spiritually and morally and ethically unsustainable, that is decaying and destroying itself?

Let's put it this way with an example provided by the early days of the pandemic:
Are you going to stay in the closed-off tomb with your 300 rolls of toilet paper, and 40 boxes of hand sanitizer, and your hoard of cash?

OR
Are you going to step out of the tomb,
into the light, and return to the land of the living, return to your friends and family, join with strangers, and start sharing your abundance,
using your energy to help others who are vulnerable and in need?

Are you going to choose to *live*
or are you going to choose to *die?*

The miracle of the gospel is that it is true for everyone.
Jesus is calling to us even if we are in the tomb,
even if we are in the tree,
even if we are in the wilderness with the devil on our backs.

The miracle of our living is that our darkness, our fear, our suffering makes the light –
which we enter when we choose to step out of the tomb –
even more beautiful.

In her book *Praying Our Goodbye*, Sister Joyce Rupp wrote about waking up to find lines of frost on her windowpanes: "We live our long, worn days in the shadows, in what often feels like barren, cold winter, so unaware of the miracles that are being created in our spirits. It takes the sudden daylight, some unexpected surprise of life, to cause our gaze to look upon a simple, stunning growth that has happened quietly inside us ... They bring us beyond life's fragmentation and remind us that we are not nearly as lost as we thought we were, that all the time we thought we were dead inside, beautiful things were being born in us."

So
what if
all those "miracles" Jesus is credited with
aren't anything more special, more significant,
more life-changing
than the kind of healing
that nourishes us, sustains us, uplifts us, renews us,
and motivates us?

The kind of healing that says
I see you
I hear you
I feel you
I'm here for you
to support you, encourage you,
to be strong when you can't be,
to be quiet when there are no words,
to be the hand you hold
when that's the touch that truly heals your spirit.

By taking care of each other,
sacrificing our own needs and comforts for others,
by looking out for our neighbours, by doing what keeps us
in right relationship with each other,

by welcoming into our lives those who are struggling,
those who are entombed by their past or their past choices,
those who experience social distance
for reasons other than a nasty virus,
we commit ordinary, everyday
yet very radical and miraculous
acts of love.

And there is no greater miracle we can witness
than the healing power of love.

N is for Noise

Peace. It does not mean to be in a place where there is no noise, trouble or hard work. It means to be in the midst of those things and still be calm in your heart.
— UNKNOWN

Many of us struggle with a lot of noise in our heads.

It's safe to say, right now, these days, we're being bombarded by information –
news channels that we can't help but tune into several times a day,
articles and videos and memes in our social feeds,
emails from our friends and families.

There are a lot of people –
reporters, writers, musicians, pastors, politicians,
just to name a few –
who are doing a lot of talking.
Some of it's helpful, some of it's entertaining,
some of it's alarming, even enraging.
Some of us may be spending far too much time
staring at a screen,
absorbing far more information and images and sounds than ever before,
listening to all sorts of different voices like never before.

And it's not good for us.
We may call it "staying informed" and "staying connected"
but it's simply not good for us —
for our minds, for our bodies, for our spirits.

Noise is the opposite of peace.
Noise is the opposite of stillness.
Noise is the opposite of silence.

We've come to believe we need to be hearing stuff
all the time —
music, news, people talking.
We spend a lot of time listening to other people,
and thinking they are right,
that they know what they're talking about,
and what they're saying is what we should be doing,
and if we're not doing it —
we're no good.

We believe we need other people to tell us what to do and
how to do it.
But the truth is: there is only one voice we need to hear.
Our own voice. Our God-connected, holy energized voice.

Because that is the only voice that knows us.

We've become so accustomed to noise that we forget what
quiet sounds like:
It sounds like our heartbeat.

It sounds like our breath.
It sounds like our soul's voice.

We've become so accustomed to noise that we forget what quiet feels like:
It feels like our heartbeat.
It feels like our breath.
It feels like … home.
Where we are free, where we are safe, where we are who we really are.

As God intended us to be. Authentic and worthy and loved.

An article in *Maclean's* magazine in 2012 suggested that taking time for introspection is key to getting over the hurdles of life, but that time is missing in the lives of most university and college students: "Students aren't left alone with their thoughts on the bus to school or the walk across campus. They're texting, listening to music, checking social media, often all at once. There's no time to mull over difficult, complicated emotions."

Now that we have a computer that fits in our hands,
when we can fill moments of stillness
with a video, a game, a text,
when we shove buds into our ears to keep out the world around us,
we rarely get a chance to clear the noise from our heads.

Psalm 46 gives us a reason to turn off the news, turn off the computer, turn off the chatter:
"Be still, and know that I am God."

How do we know who we really are, and what we are really called to do if we can't be still –
be quiet –
be present in the presence of God –
in the company of the quiet, still voice inside us longing to be heard?

"Silence is essential," said Thich Nhat Hanh, a Buddhist monk from Vietnam. "We need silence, just as much as we need air, just as much as plants need light. If our minds are crowded with words and thoughts, there is no space for us."

I walk a lot, and I walk alone and without a phone.
There is nothing in my ears but the sound of my footsteps crunching, my blood pumping,
and my breath puffing.
This is how I work out most of my problems.
It's most helpful when writing, to get out and clear out all the thoughts jumbled in my head,
then return with some thread of an idea untangled, an editor's suggestions accepted.

But last spring, as I walked into the woods behind our home,

something happened.
I felt something at the same time I realized something.
It felt like the gentlest kind of "pop" inside.
Not something I felt physically, but something I felt spiritually.
And I realized it was a seed germinating,
and I understood –
not with my brain but with my heart –
this feeling, this realization
was a seed that had been planted
deep into the cold, clay soil
when I first arrived in Nova Scotia.
It had been waiting for the right time …
and something I'd done had triggered its germination.
My feeling was that it was starting to grow.
And all I had to do
was leave it alone.

It was a feeling and a realization that was both scary and exciting.
I didn't know what the seed was, I had no idea what plant was going to emerge
(although you might be holding it in your hands right now)
but
if I hadn't been walking in silence along the old muddy road as usual,
not really thinking about anything, just breathing
and being in a state of mental and spiritual stillness …

I wouldn't have felt that pop or heard my heart explain it to me.

If we are surrounded by noise all the time,
we can't hear those small, quiet messages in our hearts;
we can't feel the tiny but fierce seeds of our spirit opening up inside us;
we can't find the courage to trust in those messages, in those pops.

We sometimes feel we can't let ourselves rest in stillness because we don't want to face whatever truth comes up.
We are afraid of rest, stillness, silence
because that is where the truth of our hearts, of our lives, is found.

Truth is hard (even when it's good). Truth means change. Truth means turmoil.
Massive or just a quiver, it's a soulquake that rocks our own personal world.

So we surround ourselves with noise to avoid hearing the truth from our heart, our voice. In her latest memoir, *This One Wild Life*, Angie Abdou writes about heading down the backside of a mountain on a hike and walking into the absence of noise: "The intensity of the deep silence combined with the infinite expansiveness of nature so moves me that I nearly cry."

In our modern world, finding stillness needs to be intentional.
The path to peace is to step away from the noise –
to take time away from the television and the iPad,
from Facebook and the phone.
Step outside or sit down alone and inhale deeply.
To breathe in and breathe out slowly until
our shoulders drop away from our ears
and our back muscles relax.
Still our bodies,
still our minds.

How about the story of Jesus' entry into Jerusalem?
You know the one –
he arrived on a donkey and the crowd went wild and they shouted Hosanna.
You can imagine the din, right?
The shouting, the calling out, the noise of it all.
Like the home team showing up on the court for the championship game.
You can't hear yourself think.
You can't catch your breath.

Jesus was surrounded by noise wherever he went.
Crowds shouting, priests demanding answers, people wanting him to heal their loved ones.
And Jesus gives us the example of how to deal with all this noise:

He went off by himself – to be still.
To be still and hear his own heart.
To be still and connect with God.

God isn't the money and the fame and crowds
chanting your name.
God isn't the television ratings and the millions
of followers.
God isn't the entourage and the loyal assistant.

God is the gentle pop of a seed emerging,
the subtle sign for a path leading your life
in a new direction,
the soft word whispered in the night that gives you hope.
God is ... *your heart.*

That's what you hear and feel and see
when you shut down all the noise
around you and inside you
and let the only sound in your head
in your heart
in your soul
be your own voice.

O IS FOR Outcasts and Oddballs

What sets you apart can sometimes feel like a burden and it's not. A lot of the time, it's what makes you great.
— EMMA STONE

My father was a funeral director so my sister and I grew up above a funeral home. Across the side street was a two-storey building that had businesses on street level with apartments above.

A girl my age named Nancy lived in one of those apartments with her grandmother.
As a child of eight, that didn't mean anything to me, but now as an adult, I know that likely meant Nancy's life was complicated.
Because we were neighbours and went to the same school, Nancy and I played together.
What I remember best about Nancy is that I wasn't nice enough to her.
I thought she was weird
because she was bigger than I was –
in a way that means she might have grown up to be a statuesque, well-built woman –
and she was loud –
in a way that means she might have grown up to be a vivacious, charismatic woman.

Or that she died of a drug overdose at the age of 19,
or didn't finish high school because she had a baby and
worked double shifts cleaning the hospital where she knew
the name of every patient,
or that she became a really successful real estate agent and
took care of her grandmother.

Because it appears she had a complicated life, all scenarios
are possible.

All I know is I probably missed out on the opportunity to
have an amazing lifelong friend because
I thought Nancy was an oddball
so I treated her like an outcast.

In order to write about Jesus' life and ministry,
I am constantly taking a long hard look at myself
because I don't like hypocrites –
therefore I don't want to be one.
And until I was a young adult,
with a loooooong learning curve of life experiences
through my 20s and 30s,
I was just as judgy and close-minded and foolish
as a person can be.

I did what we all do, at every age: I decided Nancy was too
loud, too awkward,
too needy, too pushy to be my friend.
She made me uncomfortable.

I never saw the inside of Nancy's grandmother's apartment, but I also don't remember inviting Nancy into my house to play or eat,
or even to a birthday party.
Just imagine if I had not worried about who and what was cool,
if I had just been more "Jesusy" –
at the ripe old age of eight –
and welcomed Nancy into my life as a neighbour, a playmate, a friend.
Because perhaps Nancy needed
my friendship and my family,
a welcoming place to land every so often.

But then again, maybe she didn't. Maybe this is just my regret and ego speaking.
Maybe Nancy and her grandmother were doing just fine.
Maybe Nancy was better off not having a judgy, close-minded, foolish person as a friend.

What I know now is
(because this is what we do in our 40s and 50s, isn't it?
We remember people and events we haven't thought of in decades
and we get to address our mistakes and regrets publicly)
that even if,
and especially if,
Nancy was an outcast and oddball,

I should have considered *myself* blessed
to have Nancy want to be my friend.

Blessed are you who are poor, Jesus said.
Blessed are you who are hungry, Jesus said.
Blessed are you who weep, Jesus said.
Blessed are you when people hate you, Jesus said.
Blessed are you whose lives are complicated.

If we are followers of Jesus —
if we believe that Jesus is the way, the truth, and the life —
if we heard his commandment "to love one another as I have loved you" —
then who are "we" when we look at others and say they aren't "like us"?

The word choice for the letter O comes from Rachel Held Evans' book *Searching for Sunday: Loving, Leaving, and Finding the Church*.
"This is what God's kingdom is like:
a bunch of outcasts and oddballs gathered at a table,
not because they are rich or worthy or good,
but because they are hungry, because they said yes.
And there's always room for more."

Because with love, anything is possible.
With compassion, justice, mercy,

forgiveness, kindness, fairness, and with grace –
anything is possible.

What are we hungry for?
What are we saying yes to?

Whether we have lots of money or not enough,
live in a big house or a small apartment,
have a really nice car or need public transit to get around,
can buy whatever we want when we see it
or still have to put money aside every month until we've saved enough,
whether we seem to have it all, have it together,
have no regrets,
we are all hungry for something –
we are all yearning to say yes to something.

What is it that we are hungry for,
and yearning to say yes to,
that makes all of us outcasts and oddballs,
that makes us sit down at the table with everyone else,
that makes us create the kin-dom of God here on earth?

Love. Friendship.
Welcome. Hospitality.
Peace. Sanctuary.

We are all hungry for, and saying yes to, that place where we belong – just as we are.

In our weirdness, in our uncomfortableness,
in our awkwardness,
with our glaring imperfections and our foolishness.

Where we belong is with those who make us feel welcome,
who allow us to be ourselves
and who never judge us for our "normal,"
who feed our spirits and fill our hearts
with laughter and courage,
who look at the line outside the door and see the outcasts and oddballs
and who push the people who actually remembered their invitations out of the way to say,
"Come on in! Everyone is welcome! Sit at the table!
Have something to eat and something to drink.
Here's a tissue.
Don't worry about what those people think."

How radical!
Just like Jesus, who said, "Love one another as I have loved you."

And how did Jesus love? With his heart and his body, with his mind and his spirit.
He shared his spirit ... so that we would know how to love each other.
He offered his body ... so that we would remember to treat others the way we want to be treated.

He spoke with his heart ... so that we would always hear his voice in the chaos.

A church – the building, the sanctuary, the space –
is supposed to be a place for the outcasts and oddballs.
Jesus calls us to set a table for everyone,
to welcome everyone who is hungry and yearning.

But you know there are rules, right?
It's one thing to say everyone is welcome
until they walk onto the carpet with their dirty boots,
until they sit in your regular pew,
until they swipe a can of beans off the table where we put the donations to the food bank.

Jesus says this is where they belong –
not just in this place but in our space –
in our lives.
And if you aren't showing up to say yes to Jesus' way, then why are you here?
If you aren't poor
if you aren't hungry
if you aren't weeping
if you aren't rejected and excluded and ignored
if you aren't persecuted
if you aren't an outcast and an oddball
then why are you here?

Listen:
we're not here to be pretty,
or perfect,
to show the world our shiny pews and glowing stained-glass windows,
to make the perfect pancakes on Shrove Tuesday
and sing every note perfectly.

We're here to love and to be loved.
To welcome and to be welcomed.
To show kindness and to be shown kindness.
To live and to let live.

We aren't worthy of love and mercy and grace because we do everything right,
because we never make a mistake, never say the wrong thing, never fall on our faces.

We are worthy of love and mercy *because* we get it wrong, *because* we fail, *because* we are weird and wonderful, and don't fit in,
because we are outcasts and oddballs.

Because we have experienced a pandemic that turned our lives –
as we knew them –
and our world – as we knew it –
upside down and inside out –
and it's very possible nothing will ever be the same again.

AND THAT IS THE WHOLE POINT OF JESUS,
of his life and his ministry and his death.
To turn the world upside down and inside out and leave it different than it was before.

That's also the whole point of Easter.
Not finding the Easter Bunny and hunting for chocolate eggs and wearing new outfits,
but leaving the darkness and coming back to life with a whole new way of thinking about ourselves and each other and the world.

Because the final words Jesus spoke to his long-time friends and followers before his betrayal and arrest, before they knew he would die, were these:
"I give you a new commandment, that you love one another. Just as I have loved you, you also should love one another" (JOHN 13:34, NRSV).

And that's not meant to be some abstract or generic "love,"
but a love "just as I have loved you":
compassionate and tangible, as he showed them in everything he did.

That's why being radical and weird and loud,
making people uncomfortable and forcing them to look at the way they are living
makes Jesus the greatest outcast and oddball of all times.

The kind that makes room at the table
for my long-lost friend Nancy –
and eventually, for me.

That's why the world needs outcasts and oddballs,
and of course, more Jesus.

P IS FOR Pandemic, Poverty, Privilege

Overcoming poverty is not a gesture of charity.
It is an act of justice.
— NELSON MANDELA

Some letters of the alphabet have a plethora of possibilities when it comes to choosing a word to write about.

P is one of those letters.
Obviously, the first word that came to mind was Peace.
There are a lot of scripture verses about peace.
Or Pain. Christians are very good at pain.
And Prayer.
How about Prophets? We love our prophets. Until they say stuff we don't like, then we crucify them. Which brings us back to pain.

Then there is Parable, and who did Jesus like to tell parables about?
The poor.
Ah, yes. Poverty.
Apparently – and I'm not the one who counted – in the Bible, there are the more than 250 verses on the proper use of wealth and more than 300 verses on our responsibility to care for the poor and work for justice.

There are only seven passages that refer to homosexuality, which might suggest what the major theme of the Bible is: Not who we love – but *how* we love one another.

Then it hit me: A global pandemic was declared, and those living in poverty were the hardest hit.
So how do those who are privileged deal with that?

In three of the four gospels – Matthew, Mark, and John – the same message from Jesus is recorded: "The poor will always be among you."
Is Jesus telling us we don't have to worry about poverty? That we can just ignore the poor because there's nothing we can do?

Knowing Jesus – not likely.
So what did Jesus mean by stating bluntly that there will always be poor people in our society?

According to Craig Greenfield, a Canadian poverty activist and the author of the book *Subversive Jesus*, what Jesus actually meant is the opposite of what the verse sounds like he meant.
Greenfield believes Jesus was actually advocating *generosity* and *action to eradicate poverty*, rather than hands-up-in-the-air, shoulder-shrugging apathy.

Knowing Jesus – of course he was.

Since he was Jewish, and preaching among Jewish people, since the "new testament" wasn't even a thing in Jesus' day – right? – he likely quoted a well-known passage from the Torah, specifically from the book of Deuteronomy:
"If anyone among you should become poor, don't harden your heart or close your hand against your family or friend, but open your hand and provide what is needed. For the poor will always be with you, so give generously and don't begrudge what you share" (DEUTERONOMY 15:7–11, AUTHOR'S PARAPHRASE).

For Greenfield, reading Jesus' words in their original context helps us see that his words were meant to encourage generosity towards the poor.
Jesus is reinforcing that the command to be open-handed comes from God.

What we've done, in our modern times,
is twist Jesus' words to justify apathy and tight-fistedness.
But the command in either Bible –
Hebrew or Christian –
in either cultural context –
then and now –
is clear: Open wide your hand.
Give generously and don't begrudge what you share.

So … what do those words mean during a pandemic?

Here are two headlines from mid-April 2020, just at the start of the pandemic, when we were locked in our homes, isolated from everyone, including extended family, not attending church, and totally focused on what was going on in Canada and the United States.

Headline one:
Coronavirus could push half a billion *more* people into poverty globally, UN warns
(That's in addition to the estimated three billion people who lived in poverty *before* the pandemic, according to OXFAM.)

Headline two:
The pandemic is ravaging the world's poor, even if they're untouched by the virus

A graphic circulated on Facebook during the initial pandemic lockdown that was meant to remind some of us how fortunate we were:
"How privileged are so many that, during a global pandemic, we can just stay warm at home, reading, working, still being educated, creating, talking to our loved ones, with little worries and a fridge stocked with food?"

So the pandemic hit those living in poverty the hardest, forcing them to endure the most suffering and loss –
in the same way natural disasters hit the poor the hardest and cause them the most suffering and loss.

It was the same when the vaccination rollout began; the poorest areas of Toronto became the hot spots for the virus yet they were not the first to receive vaccines.
The working poor, those considered essential workers but who didn't work in health care, were not given first dibs on their shots.

Just as Jesus knew they would be.

Privilege means some of us weren't really impacted by the pandemic – not really, not in terms of suffering and loss, in terms of a primal fear of our future and how we will survive.
The privileged were simply inconvenienced.

Katie Smith, a writer and musician living in Toronto, published an article online about being plunged into poverty when the quarantine started and she lost 40 percent of her income.
She had money set aside in an emergency fund – and that gave her an extra $140 to stock up for two weeks.
She was at the grocery store, ready to check out, and the people in front of her spent more than $800 on supplies while bragging that they could survive for months.
Meanwhile, she tallied every purchase on her calculator.

"I couldn't find high-demand items like wipes, hand sanitizer, bread, and flour," Katie wrote about shopping at the beginning of the lockdown. "Nor could I afford the jacked-up prices for toilet paper at my local store ... I walked out of there empty handed. I managed to purchase a few extra items from a different shop and dropped supplies off for the food bank. They need it more than we do."

Wait a minute –
she tapped her emergency funds in order to stock up for two weeks
but still bought supplies for the food bank?

Remember the man who ran up to Jesus wanting to know how to inherit eternal life?
Jesus told him, "Go, sell what you own, and distribute the money to the poor, and you will have treasure in heaven; then, come and follow me" (LUKE 18:22, NRSV).
When he heard this, the man was shocked and walked away upset because he had a lot of really nice stuff.

If you were told to give up everything you own except what would fit in a large plastic tote,
would you resist?
Would you walk away "to think about it"?
I know I would. I'd have to sit around – surrounded by all my stuff – and adjust to the idea.
It might take a few days.
Or a lifetime.

Those of us who have plenty tend to hold on to our abundance

because we are afraid of losing it, of having nothing.
Yet a woman who had very little managed to give to others whose need was greater than hers.

Jesus says, Sell everything you own,
give the money to the poor
THEN come and follow me.

This is the parable of the pandemic. The new parable of the poor and the privileged.
(I'm sure Jesus doesn't mind if I update his parables. Honest. I asked him. "Fill yer boots," he said.)

Here are two more headlines, from six months and one year after the official declaration of the pandemic.

Headline one:
COVID-19 to add as many as 150 million extreme poor by 2021

Headline two:
Poverty soared to a pandemic high last month

So, actually, this is the parable for AFTER the pandemic, when things do *not* return to "normal" for many people.
When our "new normal" includes
more people living in poverty
as we adjust to the job losses

and the long-term fluctuations of the job market
as businesses slowly re-open – or don't re-open at all.

We have no idea how the pandemic is going to impact the poor of the world,
the poor in our country,
and the poor in our community.

But we can start now to act as if we do. Because really, those headlines? We know.

What can we do? Three simple things:
Be grateful.
Be aware.
Be generous.

We must not take our privilege –
our abundance and our comfort and our ease –
for granted.
We must keep our eyes and ears open to what is happening around us.
And we must respond – by being open-handed.

During the pandemic, we did a great job
of taking care of each other,
of loving our neighbours,
of supporting the poor,
but we must respond – gratefully and generously – after,

when the real impact hits and the suffering and losses reveal themselves.
Reveal they will always be with us.

Open our hands.
Let our abundance flow.

Sell what you don't need and give that money to the poor, then you can follow Jesus.

The pandemic showed us what is most essential to our living.
The pandemic showed us why Jesus calls us to be kind and merciful and humble.
Why he commanded us to "love one another just as I loved you."

Why he offers the kin-dom of God to the poor and the hungry and the persecuted.

Q IS FOR Questions

A very powerful question may not have an answer at the moment it is asked. It will sit rattling in the mind for days or weeks as the person works on an answer. If the seed is planted, the answer will grow. Questions are alive.
— FRAN PEAVEY, SOCIAL ACTIVIST

When I made my early notes for each letter, brainstorming words and related scriptures, researching ideas, the word I chose for Q was questions, and it appeared it would link up nicely with Doubt.
After all, the word "question" comes from the Latin *quaerere*, which means "to seek." Questions are essential to any spiritual journey because they challenge our minds, our hearts, our beliefs, and our assumptions.
And when we are doubting and questioning, we certainly are seeking answers, because we appreciate certainty; we like to have the ground under our feet firm, the path clearly marked.

Tragedy has a way of undoing our certainty,
of liquifying the ground we stand on,
of providing more questions than answers,
of leaving us doubting and questioning
and seeking solace and hope and comfort and healing.

A little over halfway through the "Alphabet of Faith" sermon series, on Saturday April 18 and Sunday April 19, Canada's worst massacre happened in rural Nova Scotia. Twenty-two people, as well as an unborn baby, were killed overnight and into the next morning, all of them by the same man – some who knew him as their neighbour, others for whom he was a stranger, and one police officer for whom he was the suspect.

Although I did not personally know any of the victims, it happened very close to home.
Several victims were killed "just down the road," as we say in a rural area.
What stays with me is the fact I didn't know what was happening.
I went to bed on Saturday night and got up Sunday morning not knowing.
We had coffee and breakfast then Mother and I drove into town to the church.
We did the online service, including a sermon on the letter P, and a community prayer centred on peace, and returned home to fresh cups of coffee.
That's when I discovered that a gunman had gone on a rampage through my part of Nova Scotia, and at that point, at least a dozen people were dead.

The following Sunday, the letter was Q for which the word and the scriptures were already decided. Q is for Questions, and the gospel reading told the story of followers of

Jesus meeting a stranger on the road to Emmaus
(LUKE 24:13–31).

There are questions in that story we can relate to:
"How can you not know what happened?"
"How can you not know why we are so sad?"
"How can you be our Lord?"

For those two followers of Jesus, the whole concept of moving beyond grief seemed beyond them in the rawness of their sorrow and loss.
They were full of questions –
as we all are in the aftermath of any tragedy,
particularly a mass shooting perpetrated by one individual.

The first one being: Why?
Why did this happen?
In the initial weeks and months after the mass shooting, the answers to that question came slowly as the RCMP released information and timelines, and details that were appalling and horrifying, and that made us shake our heads as we whispered, "Why?"

Which leads us to a deeper, more spiritual question: How could this have happened?
With the killer dead, with the incomprehensible scope of his rampage, we will never know the answer to that question.

Or to this one: How do those who survived in the tiny community of Portapique, where the worst of the carnage occurred, move on, when their "little piece of heaven" now reminds them of eight hours of pure hell?
How do those who lost family and friends and neighbours to the randomness of the killer's actions move on?
How do those people who saw him drive by, walk up to the house next door, appear on their house-cams, live with the reality that it could have been them, as well?
Even just trying to figure out some kind of answer makes our minds – and spirits – twist into knots.

Perhaps the biggest question we ask after a mass shooting, or a preventable tragedy that happens because of a bad decision or carelessness,
is about forgiveness.

Do I have to forgive the person who did this?

Forgiveness is hard.
In our heads, we know it is healthy. Spiritually, emotionally, and mentally,
we need to forgive and let go. Forgiveness is for ourselves, for our own health.
In our hearts, however, forgiveness is not so easy.
When we are hurting, when we are missing someone who is gone because of a terrible reason, when there are questions that will never be answered, forgiveness feels impossible.

Do I have to forgive?

In the case of the mass shooting in Nova Scotia, I believe the answer is No.
This time, No. You don't have to forgive. This time, that's not our job.
Often, after violence, we speak about compassion for the person who caused the tragedy,
who killed others. Mercy for his suffering. Forgiveness for what he did.
None of that is relevant in Canada's worst mass shooting. This time, it's not our job.

Because what happened was pure evil.
Honestly, I can think of no other explanation than that: Evil.
And we don't have to deal with evil. It is beyond us. We can leave the evil up to God.
As the psalmist wrote, "For you are not a God who delights in wickedness; evil will not sojourn with you" (PSALM 5:4, NRSV).
We just have to deal with the aftermath: the destruction of lives and the pain that evil causes.

We just have to deal with the questions:
Why did this happen?
How could this have happened?
What do I know for sure?

Bad things happen, and life is suffering.
But life is also love. And love is as strong as, or even stronger, than evil.

As poet Jan Richardson says in her poem "Blessing for the Brokenhearted,"
"the only cure for love is more of it."

If we can't answer why this happened, or how could this have happened, can we answer this
question: How do we move forward through our pain and grief, our sorrow and disbelief?
How do we move through this darkness?

With *relentless love.*

The only answer to all the questions is more love.
Relentlessly.

No longer a passive love – paper hearts and fingers in the shape of a heart –
but aggressive love – compassion and kindness and mercy that look like the Hulk.
You know who I mean: big, green, muscular. Pissed off.
Big, green, growling love.

A love like that –
enflamed, enraged, emboldened –

is Jesus' command to love each other as he loved us —
on steroids.

Because that's what we need. That's what the world needs.
Relentless love.
The kind that never gives up.
Love that doesn't hold back.
Love that is resilient and courageous, and brave.
Love that doesn't think twice about
rushing over the road to help.
Love that doesn't hesitate.
Love that doesn't question.

Colchester County councillor Bob Pash, who read a short speech during the Nova Scotia Remembers vigil on the Friday night following the mass shooting,
ended his speech by saying, "I love you all."
A message to his constituents, broadcast across the province and across the nation.
No holding back.
I love you all.
Relentlessly.

Now and forever. No matter what.

The last question the disciples from the Emmaus Road asked was,

"Were not our hearts burning within us while he talked with us on the road
and opened the Scriptures to us?"

What was burning in their hearts was love. Relentless, death-defying love.

Love is the only answer to the disciples' question,
and to ours, as we move on into life after death:
What now?

R IS FOR Rest

Rest and laughter are the most spiritual
and subversive acts of all. Laugh, rest, slow down.
— ANNE LAMOTT

In 2020, it took me four months to put away the Christmas decorations that were in boxes piled up in the guest room.
As soon as I did that, I celebrated my 50th birthday and it was safe to assume the empty boxes from birthday presents would remain stacked in the dining room on Canada Day.

One of these days, the cats will trigger an avalanche of the stacks of books, papers, and notebooks in my home office and I'll be buried alive.
Oh, day of blessed rest!

Speaking of which, I can't really move the boxes out of the dining room because one of our three cats is usually sleeping in one of them.

The other day, my husband said, "You wouldn't even know how to spell 'chill out.'"
You'd think he'd be used to that by now.
But when he says it – when he finally notices – that tells me it must be bad, it must be obvious.

It tells me it's time to give myself a rest from working and instead devote at least 24 hours
to reading novels and doing puzzles.
And maybe curling up in a box for a nap.

Let me encourage you to curl up in a box of your own:

You need to rest.
You are allowed to rest.
You are allowed to stop scrolling through Facebook and Twitter and Instagram.
You are allowed to turn off your phone and your iPad, to turn off the news.
You are allowed to not watch Netflix.
You are allowed to rest.

Rest your eyes and your ears.
Your mind and your heart,
your nervous system and your spirit.
Rest. Step away, slow down. Pause. Reset. Rest.

That's so radical, isn't it? To suggest it's not only okay but advisable to rest.
Because we live in a culture where doing more is better and busyness is worn as a badge of honour: "I'm so busy!"

But in his new book, *The Comfort Book*, British author Matt Haig writes, "You don't need to be *busy*. You don't need to justify your existence in terms of productivity. Rest

is an essential part of survival. An essential part of us."
And the truth is:
Some of us are struggling to just keep up.
Some of us are finding it hard to catch our breath.
Some of us feel too burnt-out to even think about rest.

You know that feeling: "I'm too tired to sleep."
Too many of us are in survival mode. We're exhausted.
We need to rest, but we've forgotten how. We've forgotten how to be still.

But do you remember what Jesus said? "Come to me, you who are weary and burdened, and I will give you rest."
Or put another way: "If you're tired and burnt-out, get outside. Come walk with me. I'll show you how to live."

Jesus understood.
He knew what it meant to be exhausted and stressed out, to have anxiety about … everything.
He knew how it felt to juggle meetings and people and expectations.

Of course, that's also part of his "give up your stuff" kick.
What's with that?
Does he really think giving up our possessions –
all our gadgets and vehicles, cottages and camps, tools and decorations –
will somehow help us to be calm and relaxed … and to feel rested?

Is it possible JC was the original "declutter your life" guru?
Is it possible that peace is found in less, not more?
Let's not go there. Instead, let's put on our new outfit and get in our nice big boat
and head out on the lake for an afternoon's cruise.

Remember Jesus in a boat?

We get one of the greatest metaphors of all time from Jesus hanging out in a boat.
Because what did Jesus do when the storm came up and everybody raced around trying to get their life jackets on while holding on to the railings for dear life?

Jesus napped.
In the middle of the storm, he rested.

He didn't panic and freak out
like so many of us do (hello!) when the storms of life
bear down on us.
He just stopped,
stepped away from the drama and the busyness,
waved away the To Do list,
turned off the phone,
and rested.
He went off by himself to pray,
or he leaned back in the boat and had a snooze,
or he sat down with his friends for a meal.

That dude knew how to chill. He was the first prophet of self-care.

Abby Millard, writing in the spring 2020 issue of *Ruminate* magazine, said, "Our busy and occupied lives slowly chip away at our ability to experience rest. The city never sleeps and so neither do we. When a moment of rest finally arrives, we meet it filled with restlessness. An evening or a weekend or a retirement suddenly stares us in the face and we wonder, at a loss, what our purpose should be now."

Hey, it's okay for our purpose to be rest.
To just stop. Take a break. Put yourself in a time out. To chill out.
Matt Haig also said, "I think that resting might actually be the main point of life."
Those of us who live with dogs and cats know this to be true.

After all, Jesus didn't say, "Come to me and be happy and optimistic!"
He didn't say, "Come to me and I'll find stuff for you to do!"
He said, "Come to me, no matter how distracted,
how wound up you are,
and I will give you rest."

And what happens when we rest?

The same thing that happens in stillness and peace, meditation and prayer:
We find ourselves. Our true selves. We find who we are and what our purpose should be now.
We find strength and courage and hope.
We reconnect with our breath and our heartbeat.

Rest *because* it is radical and countercultural.
Just like Jesus was.

We talk about Jesus and his "upside-down" gospel, right? Blessed are those who weep, blessed are those who hunger, blessed are those who are persecuted ...
Well, in our world, in our culture, what's more upside down than turning off, tuning out, winding down? Getting down on our knees in a garden? Having a good cry? Going to bed early? Not doing anything at all?
Blessed are those who sleep, blessed are those who take it easy, blessed are those who step away from the drama ...

Speaking of rest being essential for survival, when Christena Cleveland, Ph.D., a professor, researcher and author, wrote about her experience of needing rest in a recent Instagram post, she took it to the next level: "The thing about being a Black woman is that the world is never safe. That's why we Black women struggle to rest. We can never let our guard down. That's why believing that God is a Black woman is liberating. I can finally rest, knowing that Someone trustworthy is on the lookout."

This perspective needs to be heard.
This is a statement to accept, not question,
a statement to understand in the context of justice.
I can't write about rest and not include this truth, this challenge to basic survival.

Everyone needs to rest.
Everyone deserves rest.
Jesus invites everyone to rest.
And you know he means *everyone*.

Rest is grace. Rest is the gift, the reassurance, the response.

In the middle of the storm,
when the crowds are pressing in and
all you hear are other people's voices telling you what you should do,
when you should do it, how much you need to get done –
when you are tired of flipping tables,
when you feel overwhelmed and scared and alone,
when you feel weary and burdened,
when you need to put your guard down,
take a time out –
turn away from it all, shut it down, sign out, and
find a comfortable cushion to lay on,
say your prayers, count your blessings,
give thanks, and
rest.

S is for Seeds

That's something I've noticed about food: whenever there's a crisis, if you can get people to eating normally things get better.
— MADELEINE L'ENGLE

The gospel of Mark is the second book of the Christian scriptures, but it's believed to have been written first and used as a source for the other gospels. Mark doesn't begin with a story about Jesus' birth or his childhood, but opens with Jesus as an adult, beginning his ministry with his baptism by John.

His teachings, outlined in chapter 4, are lovely and relatable:
– seeds planted on a path get snatched up by birds
– seeds planted on rocky ground cannot take root
– seeds planted among thorns are choked away
and of course,
– seeds planted in good, fertile soil grow and produce.

The point of these parables is to answer the question, "What is the kingdom of God like?"
When Jesus says it, it's "kingdom." When I, and others, use it, we go with "kin-dom."

Reta Halteman Finger, Ph.D., writing for the online *Christian Feminism Today* magazine, says the word "kin-dom" reflects the new society Jesus envisioned: "a shared community of equals who serve each other." She does acknowledge the political context of Jesus' time when the term "kingdom" was easily understood, as well as in the 1600s when the *King James Bible* was created.

So when Jesus answers the question, "What is the kingdom of God?" he's thinking about the new society he'd like to create.

"The kingdom of God is like someone who plants seed in the ground. Night and day, whether the person is asleep or awake, the seed still grows, but the person does not know how it grows" (MARK 4:26–27, NCV).

It's easy to look at our gardens, at the fields, at a marsh, at the woods, and see the kin-dom of God growing out of those seeds – the beauty and the peacefulness, the unity and the equality. All the plants living in harmony with each other.

But what about other places in our world?

Does the kin-dom of God look like a bombed-out village?
Does it look like a mass grave?
Does it look like an enormous island of garbage floating in the ocean?

Does it look like emaciated children squatting in the dust?
Does it look like a shot-up nightclub?
Does it look like bodies lying broken on the pavement?

If those were our only answers,
if all we saw when we looked around was devastation and death and despair,
if we felt so overwhelmed by suffering that we turned away and shrugged our shoulders,
we'd be a doomed civilization, wouldn't we?
We'd be "approaching spiritual death," as Martin Luther King Jr. called it in 1967 (writing in the context of a country spending more money on the military than on social programs).

But as Earth's population grows and the messes we make get bigger,
it also means goodness and good people and good intentions are multiplying too.

Amen for that.

And the answer to the question is right in front of us, found not only in the gospel of Mark but in Matthew and Luke as well – because it's the right answer.
What is God's kin-dom like?

"It is like what happens when a mustard seed is planted in the ground. It is the smallest seed in all the world. But once it is planted, it grows larger than any garden plant. It even puts out branches that are big enough for birds to rest in its shade" (MARK 4:30–32, CEV).

Something small becomes something big. Something big provides shelter to something small.

That's kindness.
Which is another word for love.

All we are asked to do is love one another.
And our enemies.
Commands that come with no exceptions,
no asterisks,
no footnotes that provide a nice little loophole that begins with, "Unless … "

We are called to love each other.
To take care of each other. To be kind to one another.
Even the awful ones. Especially the awful ones.

American novelist Henry James put it simply:
"Three things in human life are important.
The first is to be kind.
The second is to be kind.
And the third is to be kind."

Or as the popular saying goes,
"In a world where you can be anything, be kind."

Kindness flows out of empathy and hospitality
and appreciation.
Kindness means extending a helping hand
with no expectation of anything in return.
It means being generous – with time, money, skills,
even hugs.
It means practicing forgiveness – letting go of hurt and
anger and fear and practicing Jesus' radical call for …

Love.
Also know as: Kindness. Compassion. Hospitality. Justice.

All avenues for creating God's kin-dom here on earth.

It just starts with a small seed.

You plant a seed – a smile, a casserole, a coffee – and you hope it grows.
You hope it falls into good soil where it can flourish and spread more seeds.

For five years, I lived at home with my parents because my father had Alzheimer's disease. At one point, I had a mother in the hospital with complications related to her treatment for cancer and a father in the locked unit of the nursing

home. My days started with walking the dogs, then running back and forth between the two facilities taking care of my parents.
So yeah,
there was a Friday night when my friend Shelagh phoned to check in and I was barely lucid –
exhausted both mentally and physically – but I complained, "I'm so tired of eating cold pizza."

The next morning, feeling better after a good night's sleep,
I opened our front door on my way to the farmers' market and nearly tripped over a cooler on the step.
I brought the cooler inside and opened it up. On top were two magazines and under them were some very nice chocolates. Under that was a quiche and a meat pie and some frozen veggies –
which Shelagh later told me, after I'd eaten them, were just to keep everything cool!

If the good night's sleep renewed my body,
the cooler full of food replenished my spirit.

Shelagh planted a seed that just keeps propagating, providing goodness for herself and for others.
A few years later, Shelagh told me about a friend of hers who'd had a stroke. Shelagh wanted to do something but she didn't know what. She felt she wasn't close enough with the woman to just show up at her door.

"Then I remembered the cooler of food!" Shelagh said.
Another crisis, another cooler, another spirit replenished by kindness.

On the other hand,
like a seed slipping through a crack in a concrete sidewalk
or an asphalt driveway,
taking root on rocky ground or amongst thorny bushes,
yet still sprouting where nothing should grow,
let alone flourish,
something remarkable, perhaps even surprising,
grows from a confrontation, a thoughtless comment,
or a failure.

When I was in my 20s,
I made two separate off-the-cuff remarks.
The first one was racist
and the second one was derogatory.
Both comments expressed stereotypes and were born out of ignorance, not a deliberate attempt to insult or hurt.
I didn't make them about the person who happened to be standing behind me at the moment I spoke, but about the culture they belonged to –
I'm grateful to have been exposed in that moment because, as humiliating as it was
to be caught with my foot in my mouth,
it was the best thing to happen to me.

Those seeds of shame burrowed inside me and started to grow instantly.

I carried those seeds inside me,
watered them with awareness,
fertilized them with knowledge and understanding,
until they grew into lush and healthy plants
producing the fruits of
compassion, thoughtfulness, and acceptance –
although I have yet to taste the fruit of forgiveness,
despite the moments of grace
that have otherwise blossomed.

Take a moment here for reflection, for revelation:
What small seed was planted in your life
that became a big moment –
for you or for someone else?

What small seed is planted in you
that has yet to be nurtured?

What is that idea inside you that you don't know what to do with – but feel the need to see grow into something big?

Craig Greenfield is an activist and an author who walks the talk when it comes to putting into practice the teachings of Jesus – actually living the way Jesus calls us to live. In his book *Subversive Jesus*, Craig writes about living in

Vancouver's Downtown Eastside with his family.
I'm familiar with the area since I lived in East Vancouver for a few years,
but it's a place I only saw
through the windows of the bus – safely distanced from the drug dealers and the addicts, the homeless and the mentally ill.

This is why one particular story strikes a chord in my heart. When Craig and his family and his community were struggling with how to handle the drug dealers in their neighbourhood, they put Jesus' command to "love your enemies" into practice. Instead of sending out an "enforcer" to bully the dealers away, they created a street party that ended up providing a fun and safe space –
and chocolate chip cookies –
on Welfare Wednesday, the drug dealers' busiest day.

That small seed – a street party – made a big impact on the lives of struggling addicts trying to be clean and sober, "a turning point for our block," Greenfield writes. "We had not turned that corner through force or aggression, but rather through a Spirit of vulnerability, love, celebration and joy."

Reading that story was such a WOW moment.
Maybe some of you, like me, are thinking, *Nothing I can do will compare to* that!

What can my seed do for the larger group,
for the whole world?
It's just one, small seed.

Small seeds turning into big moments of transformation and redemption
is a message we need to hear
when our hearts are broken and our ears are bleeding,
when our minds are whirling with unanswerable questions,
such as "What can *I* do?"

We don't give up.
We don't say, "It's too much for one person."
We don't say, "It's hurts too much."
We keep at it, planting those seeds and hoping at least one makes it.

Because Jesus was just one.
Sure, he had 12 disciples
(more, of course, including the women who were part of his ministry),
but he was the example, the mouthpiece,
the magnet, the target.
He was just one guy who said,
"I have a new way, a new truth, and a new life for you."
He was just one guy who said,
"Love one another as I have loved you."

He was just one guy who kept walking around
and talking to people,
helping out and healing and bringing hope where there was none;
he was one guy who just kept throwing seeds around,
knowing that a few of them would land in good soil.
And that's what makes a difference.

T is for Time

*I've decided that there's nothing better to do than
go ahead and have a good time and get the most we
can out of life. That's it — eat, drink, and make
the most of your job. It's God's gift.*
— ECCLECIASTES 3:13, MSG

Poet William Carlos Williams said, "Time is a storm in which we are all lost."

It's interesting to think of time as a storm:
Like the weather, it dictates what we do but it's not something we can control.
We can't even see time —
the reason why, when we're away from a clock,
we lose track of time.

Usually we think of time like the wind.
We can't see it, but it is there, in our lives always
influencing how we live.

Think what happens when your computer needs to be fixed or upgraded:
There's an enforced break from work,
which results in unplanned, unexpected, and perhaps
much needed downtime.

A time out.
A time to rest. A time to heal. A time to be quiet.
Which, of course, means it becomes a time to plant, a time to repair, a time to rebuild!
It becomes a time to get all those ignored chores done.

But that's all *human* time. Our plans, our goals, our work. As we keep busy, keep distracted, keep moving forward, we ignore a fact of our faith: We're actually living in God's time.

Here is part of a meditation written by Teilhard de Chardin, an early 20th-century Jesuit priest.
I keep the entire piece taped to the wall by my desk to remind me that we live and dream and work and serve in God's time. Whenever I get frustrated that my plans aren't "moving along quickly enough," I read this:

"Trust in the slow work of God.
We are, quite naturally,
impatient in everything to reach the end
without delay.
We should like to skip
the intermediate stages.
We are impatient of being
on the way to something unknown,
something new.
And yet it is the law of all progress
that it is made by passing through

some stages of instability –
and that it may take a very long time."

You know how you read something and it speaks to you in a certain way –
and years later, you read it again ... and it speaks to you in a completely different way because now your context has changed?

That's exactly what I witnessed during the early months of the pandemic and the Black Lives Matter protests – as a human, but also as a follower of the Way of Jesus: progress. It may not have felt like progress, but that's what those stages of instability gave us.

A time when we had our eyes opened to the inequalities and the inequities in the world –
like how those who provide services to us, who take care of us, who worked through the pandemic, are paid the least.
A time when we realized the long-standing crisis in our long-term care facilities
and how our most vulnerable elders –
people who can no longer fight back, or demand fairness and justice –
are *truly* treated at the hands of those who nickel and dime in order to put profit before people.

A time when we understood that "the common good" means we are called to *sacrifice* something of our lives –

a certain amount of income or freedom of movement or just the accumulation of more stuff —
in order to keep everyone safe and healthy.

My hope throughout the pandemic was that when it was over, we would understand
we had entered a time of great potential for progress —
potential we have squandered after other crises —
but —
let's be hopeful —
let's see this as moving towards
a time to plant and heal,
a time to rebuild and repair,
a time to speak up,
a time to be merciful and fair, just and equitable —
a time for peace.

A time when we truly understand what the kin-dom of God looks like, and what the way and truth of Jesus really is all about.
It can happen — if we realize *now* is the time.

Now is the time for the apocalypse.

Another word we use but may not actually understand.

Apocalypse is a Greek word meaning "revelation."
It means we're experiencing an "unveiling" or an "unfolding" of things we didn't know about before —

or chose to ignore –
things which could not be known if this unveiling –
this revelation –
hadn't taken place.

Other modern definitions speak of great destruction and violent change; widespread destruction or disaster.

Biblically, apocalypse has come to mean End of Times.
And that's where we are now, isn't it?
The global viral pandemic created
an "apocalypse" for our world –
an eye-opening experience for our 21st-century existence.
We could be at the "end of a time" of selfishness and corruption, of individualism, of greed and gross wealth.
We could be at the "end of a time" of hatred, of exclusion and discrimination, of privilege and power.
We could be at the "end of a time" of us versus them.

No wonder Jesus said, "Stay awake! Keep alert! Keep watch!"
Because the "end of times" could come at any time.

I don't mean the literal return of Jesus, but the coming of what his life and teachings, his death and resurrection were all about:
compassion, justice and mercy, kindness and fairness, balance and harmony.
All those blessings he shared on the mountain.

All the blessings of *shalom* –
peace and prosperity, wholeness, wellness and serenity –
that he grew up learning.
A time when we come together as a community and take care of each other.
A time when we love each other as he loved us – as he loved the broken and the lost, the weary and the weak, the addicted and the isolated, the anxious and the depressed.
A time when those with hungry hearts receive what they need, and the privileged go away empty-handed.

If we are brave, if we are the pure of heart, if we are the peacemakers,
we could transform our world, our culture.
The brokenness of our world –
of our political systems, our financial systems,
our welfare systems –
has been revealed to us.
The brokenness of our lives –
of our consumption, our waste, our sense of entitlement –
has been revealed to us.

We have the chance to see this as our apocalypse: our time to plant, to heal, to rebuild, to repair, to speak up, to transform. To commit ourselves to the way and the truth Jesus revealed to us.

We see, we believe.
Help our unseeing. Help our unbelieving.

As Sister Joan Chittister wrote in her book *For Everything a Season*, about Ecclesiastes 3:1–8,
"There is no such thing as being 'born out of time.'
Our time is now. The era into which we are born is the era for which we have responsibility, the era for which we are meant to be a blessing. Whatever is going on now ... is our affair."

It is time to transform our lives and our world.
This is our affair –
our apocalypse –
our revelation –
the unfolding of God's work in God's time.

And the time is now.

U is for Unity

*We are each other's harvest; we are each other's business;
we are each other's magnitude and bond.*
— GWENDOLYN BROOKS

Unity is defined as "oneness" – the state of being one.

Now, because a retired high school math teacher attended the church I served in rural Nova Scotia, I always liked to throw in something mathematical every so often because – let's be honest –
most of us don't want to talk about high school math.

In math, unity is a synonym for "number one." The number one represents a single entity and is our unit of counting.

At this point, I could have told you all about unity as an identity element, but I have no idea what any of what I read actually means, so let's just nod our heads and smile widely as if we already know all about it. Like many of us did during high school math.

What I *can* tell you about is the *value* of unity – because in this case, it has nothing to do with math.
Unity is harmony within and among individuals in the group.

Unity is built from a shared vision, a shared hope, an altruistic aim or a cause for the common good. The stability of unity comes from the spirit of equality and oneness.

Aha! There's that word: oneness. The state of being one.

Which leads to another U word:
ubuntu –
an African philosophy that translates most simply as, "I am because we are."

The following anecdote is one of those stories that has been shared so often it's impossible to attribute it with any certainty and it has simply become part of our common storytelling.

"Today I read a story about an anthropologist who proposed a game to the kids in an African tribe. He put a basket full of fruit near a tree and told the kids that who ever got there first would win the sweet fruits. When he told them to run, they all took one another's hands and ran together, then sat together enjoying their treats. When he asked them why they had run like that as one could have had all the fruits for himself, they said: 'Ubuntu. How can one of us be happy if all the other ones are sad?'"

Here's the take-away – for every day, for everyone, no matter where we live:
How can one of us be happy if all the other ones are sad?

The African concept of *ubuntu* suggests that your sense of self is shaped by your relationships with other people.
It certainly comes into direct opposition to the rampant individualism that has taken over our modern world.
Ubuntu is about how my humanity, my existence as a person, is fostered and nurtured by being in relationship with other people.
In practice, *ubuntu* means believing the common bonds within a group are more important than any individual issues within it. It's about the common good, doing what's best for the whole community, not just a few people.

Which sounds very much like Paul's interpretation of Jesus' teachings in his letter to the Galatians: "We are to use our freedom not for our own pleasures but to serve one another humbly with love" (5:13, PARAPHRASE).

Here's the thing about unity: We're all in this together.
Truly, the pandemic drove home this truth for many of us, and the time has come to embody this truth as a world, as one humanity, once and for all.

This is especially important for us as Christians because Jesus' teachings come from a universal truth: We are all in this together.
We are all people of God. We are siblings in Christ. We are one body and one Spirit.

Jesus also said, "What you do to the least among you, you do to me."
How can one of us be happy if all the other ones are sad?

Let's consider unity in the context of freedom, as mentioned in the verse from Galatians.

In an article published online in *Sojourners* magazine in May, 2020, Reverend Jes Kast wrote,
"I believe in individual rights. I believe in justice and equity and personal freedom. But freedom, scripturally, is often not just about what I want as it is about what is best for the whole community. Freedom is about responsibility for each other to live out the greatest commandment to love one another. Freedom is humble."

She went on to say, "Freedom is about the greater good of the community. Freedom is about how we ensure that we love one another and take care of one another. Freedom is not just about what I personally can and can't do. Freedom, biblically speaking, is always about the whole community, especially with how we take care of the most vulnerable."

I have to point this out: the word unity is in the word comm-unity. We can't talk about community – like a community of faith – without understanding that unity is at the heart of it.

It's also important to note this caveat about unity courtesy of a homily Pope Francis shared in 2017 about two temptations.
As related by Sarah Bessey in her book *Miracles*,
the first temptation is diversity without unity – meaning we separate ourselves into groups, we take sides, we adopt rigid positions and become locked into our own ideas and ways of doing things.
That's one way to lose freedom.
The second temptation is unity without diversity – that's uniformity where everyone has to conform and become the same.
That's another way to lose freedom.

So unity is about love and humility, *ubuntu* and the common good, acceptance and inclusion:
I am because we are.
I am free because we are free.
I am happy because we are happy.
I am healthy because we are healthy.

We belong in and long for community –
we live and work best
when we are in relationship with others –
when we are fostering relationships that support and uplift and honour the spirit of others –
when we are serving others humbly with love.

In the spring of 2020, Canadian writer and radio producer Tara Henley published a book called *Lean Out: A Meditation on the Madness of Modern Life.*

One of the chapters near the end of the book is called "The Commons," and in it, Henley writes about where her quest to understand modern life has taken her:

"It led me here, to the most pressing issue of our time: economic inequality. Underlying every single issue that I'd explored – from food culture to transportation – was the reality that we live in a massively unequal society."

When we think of unity, of being united, we must think in terms of the common good, of freedom for everyone, of serving others with humility and love.

We are not here to serve our own pleasures –

to hoard toilet paper, to put gates around our communities, to put our money into offshore accounts in order to avoid paying taxes, to put jobs and the economy ahead of the health and safety of our essential workers and our vulnerable citizens.

We are here to serve others – humbly, lovingly, gently, and patiently.

Dr. Martin Luther King, Jr. said, "In a real sense, all life is interrelated. All people are caught in an inescapable network of mutuality, tied in a single garment of destiny. What affects one directly, affects all indirectly."

After all, how can one of us be happy if all the other ones are sad?

V is for Vision

*Give to us clear vision that we may know
where to stand and what to stand for – because
unless we stand for something,
we shall fall for anything.*

— PETER MARSHALL, U.S. SENATE CHAPLAIN, 1947

Are you someone who sees the glass as half empty
or as half full?
Are you someone who sees the good in people,
or do you become fixated on one flaw, one misdeed?
Are you someone who sees something wrong and works to
fix it, or who shrugs and figures,
what's the point, it's not going to change anything?

What do you see?

Vision isn't just the physical sight we have –
it's also our values, and our personal plan for what is most
important in life.
This applies to each of us as individuals, but also to all of
us as a community of faith –
our common values and our common plan for what is most
important as followers of Jesus living in the 21st century.

If the season of Lent asks us to look inside ourselves and to reflect on how we are living, then the season of Pentecost – which begins with a reminder that we are disciples of Jesus, in a world that needs more Jesus – asks us to look around ourselves and see how our living affects others.

What is your vision of the world,
when fires are burning in cities across the United States because of generations of fear and pain, racism and discrimination, hatred and violence?
When billionaires and children living in poverty exist at the same time?

What is your vision of your life
when we are asked to stop, look at, and listen to the suffering of others?
When we are asked to look at the world through someone else's eyes and to see what they see?

Most importantly, what is Jesus' vision for the world
when the current systems of government and justice, health care and education and welfare are being revealed as flawed and inequitable, as exclusive and unfair?

Jesus wanted a revolution that would create a new system, a new order of mercy, justice, and humility, where those who suffer –
those who mourn –

those who try to make peace –
come out on top.
Jesus wanted to turn the world upside down –
so the meek are strong and the hungry are fed
and the persecuted are respected.

There's something that needs to be pointed out concerning vision:

Jesus used the metaphor of "blindness" and we interpret these teachings as being about *spiritual* blindness. Like when he says in the gospel of Luke, "God has sent me to proclaim freedom for the prisoners and recovery of sight for the blind, to release the oppressed … "
He's not talking about a literal curing of a physical blindness – but about a new way of seeing.

The danger in this, and it's the same danger we encounter when we speak about darkness and black, is *our* tendency to be literal.
This makes physical blindness a negative thing.
Something that is bad, wrong, diminished, lacking.
Something that needs to be cured or fixed in order for a person to be whole.

Yet blindness and darkness are preferred metaphors for how many of us live and act – or don't act – as people of faith in the world.

One of America's pre-eminent Christian writers, Barbara Brown Taylor, writes in her book *Learning to Walk in the Dark* that perhaps seeing has made her blind: "by giving me cheap confidence that one quick glance at things can tell me what they are, by distracting me from learning how the light inside me works, by fooling me into thinking I have a clear view of how things really are, of where the road leads, of who can see rightly and who cannot."

Brown Taylor's book explores how darkness is not something to fear, but something we all need – both the literal darkness and the spiritual darkness.
We need to experience the dark and sit with the truth that is revealed to us.

But we don't like to see the dark things, the hard things, the things that make us uncomfortable – like a black man held down and begging for breath, while a knee is pressed into his neck;
a black man gunned down while jogging;
the body of a 15-year-old Indigenous girl, wrapped in a blanket, pulled from a river;
asylum seekers crowded into a boat that capsizes in the seas;
asylum seekers separated from their children at the border and held in immigration detention centres.

"I just can't watch the news anymore," we say, "it's so upsetting. It makes me uncomfortable."

We say, "I don't want to see."
When we choose not to see the hard stuff, to see what is happening to others, to see our role in what is happening –
and our role in how to change it –
when we turn the other cheek only so that we don't have to see any more –
we have lost our vision.
We have lost our voice.
We have lost our purpose.

Nothing changes if we refuse to see. Systems don't change, revolutions don't happen, Jesus doesn't fulfill his promise if we refuse to see, if we choose not to act on our vision –
our common values and our common mission.
Which is, as always, to love one another through justice and mercy and kindness and peace.

Author and blogger Ann Voskamp wrote on Facebook about remaining silent, and I've tweaked her statement to reflect this idea of vision:
"When we *refuse to see* the face of injustice, we loudly slap the face of God. Because the person being abused is the face of God."

Here's a final question:
If you don't watch the news because it's upsetting,
if you turn away because it makes you uncomfortable,
how do you feel about following a man
who was *crucified* –

one of the most horrific kinds of deaths –
because he did *not* remain silent?
Because he believed in his values and his mission?

Because he saw the world upside down?
Because his vision
included all the realities we prefer to turn a blind eye to?

I see.
Help my unseeing.

W is for Wilderness

True belonging is the spiritual practice of believing in and belonging to yourself so deeply that you can share your most authentic self with the world and find sacredness in both being a part of something and standing alone in the wilderness.
— BRENÉ BROWN

The season of Lent begins with the story of Jesus going into the wilderness after his baptism but before beginning his ministry.
He spent 40 days in the wilderness, or desert,
as a kind of cleanse –
ridding his body of its knowledge of his previous life
and resetting his default settings
by resisting the temptations of hunger, personal power, and possessions.

If we think of wilderness literally, it means a place far from any human civilization and distraction.
A place that is unpredictable and harsh, offering nothing but hardship and the possibility of death.
To be in the wilderness puts us at the mercy of forces beyond our control.

The wilderness is a void – an abyss – an empty space.

The wilderness represents separation from what is familiar and safe.
It means feeling lost and overwhelmed.
It means isolation and aloneness.

Biblically, the wilderness is a desert, a place containing the barest minimum to support life.
The desert is the landscape of the ancestors of our faith.

For us, the wilderness also is a forest or a mountain landscape, or even a beach.
For some, the wilderness can be a one-bedroom apartment in a new city or a solo road trip across the country.
It is simply any place where we are or feel we are isolated, on our own, stripped down to the barest minimum – where we must do the work in order to understand ourselves on our life's journey.
Why am I here? What am I supposed to do, to learn?

This environment is all about getting us to answer the questions that arise as soon as we enter the wilderness.

Who will we be and what will we do when we leave the wilderness?
Will we have found new life by facing our demons?
Or will we perish because we refused to try; because we

refused to face harsh, unrelenting truths; because we refused to do things differently?

American author, environmentalist, and anarchist Edward Abbey, said, "Wilderness is not a luxury but a necessity of the human spirit."

Wilderness comes across as an ominous entity, a place of darkness and fear and hardship –
of possible death –
but just as we need the darkness, just as the darkness is essential for spiritual enlightenment,
we need the wilderness.

According to Rabbi Annie Lewis of the Germantown Jewish Centre in Philadelphia, wilderness "is a place of uncertainty and expansiveness, of majesty and possibility. When we make ourselves like a wilderness, we open our hearts and minds to being changed by what we encounter."

And it's more than a season of the church,
more than a religious experience;
we encounter the wilderness all the time.
Wilderness is an ongoing human experience.

Raise your hand if you know someone who has just embarked on a long journey through the wilderness of grief. We all understand how our friend or relative feels. We've

all experienced the gut-wrenching, soul-hollowing-out grief
of losing someone we love – but we also know
she goes into that wilderness alone.

I recently experienced the wilderness as a void –
a feeling of not knowing what my future looked like.
I knew I had a future,
but I had no idea what I would be doing.
I experienced this void as a physical presence, not tangible,
but present –
and I knew I simply had to continue to walk the path I was on, alongside this void –
through this wilderness of not knowing –
and be curious about what might be at the end of the void.
For I trusted there was an end.

My curiosity was my hope that there *was* life, a future, after the void – that I would walk out of the wilderness at some point.

Poet Robert Frost said, "Hope is not a way out but a way through."
Because when we step into, or are thrown into,
the wilderness –
for who among us really chooses to be in the wilderness? –
when we enter the wilderness,
there is only getting through it.

Unlike all the search-and-rescue advice we get
about what to do
if we find ourselves lost in the woods –
remain in one place,
wait to be found –
in a spiritual wilderness,
we have to keep going.
We can't stop
moving
believing
hoping
praying.

We enter into the wilderness on a daily,
monthly, yearly basis.

Grief and loss are the big ones – and they cover a lot of experiences.
The death of a loved one, or the end of a marriage.
Being fired from a job,
or receiving a life-changing diagnosis.

The anniversary of a loved one's death, or their birthday, is often a *day* of being in the wilderness. When we sit with our pain and our sorrow, our joy and our memories, and we are just there, for that day. A day to get through. And each time, we get stronger, more resilient. That particular wilderness gets a little easier to handle each time we enter it and accept it and go through it.

Change is also a wilderness.
The Black Lives Matter protests are a wilderness in which we fight against the temptation of systemic racism, of otherism, of us versus them.

The Black Lives Matter movement –
and indeed, all awareness of
the oppression of people of colour –
is changing –
transforming –
our world and our lives as we know them.

And that is the work of the wilderness:
To make you ask yourself, why am I resisting?
What am I afraid of?
Why am I defensive about thinking and speaking and behaving and relating in new,
more inclusive, more loving ways?
Why am I not comfortable with others having the same opportunities and rewards as I enjoy?

Change is not easy for some folks, particularly folks of certain ages, generations, and skin colour.
They don't want change at the best of times – Excuse me, you're sitting in my pew – but tell them the system they know so well
is wrong?
That gets a few backs up.
That gets the "I'm too old for this crap" face.

That gets the "I know all that, but ..." reply that is like nails on a chalkboard.

Resistance to change is futile.
The times, they are a-changin'. Finally. And it's wild, baby.

Remember the prayer that Jesus taught: *Your kingdom come on earth ...*
Well, the time has come.

This is truly Jesus' time: Time for a revolution.
Time for the upside-down gospel.
Time for those who hunger and thirst for justice.
Time for the peacemakers.
Time for those who have been persecuted and oppressed and killed.

Ultimately, the wilderness is about acquiring wisdom and understanding.
About being broken open – and being open to what rushes into that space.

And we must do the work –

we must do the walk through the wilderness
in order to discover
this wisdom,
this understanding,
this openness.

We must accept change and be part of it.
Otherwise, we get left behind.

We must make the journey through the wilderness,
each of us, by ourselves –
with support, with friendship,
with books and online videos,
with marches and vigils and speeches,
with food left on the doorstep –
otherwise, we never truly gain insight
into our spiritual path.

The wilderness is intensely personal at the same time as it
is universal and ancient.
It is in our DNA.

Wilderness is an unavoidable part of human existence,
just as change is.
To ignore, to resist, to deny
is to create misery
and to miss opportunity.

Wilderness is necessary.
Stay in it.
Accept it.
Trust it.
Learn from it.
Be transformed by it.

Believe you are stronger than you feel.

As Cheryl Strayed wrote in her memoir, *Wild*, about hiking alone on the Pacific Crest Trail,
"I was amazed that what I needed to survive could be carried on my back. And most surprising of all, I could carry it."

And, as with any hike through the wilderness, what we carry on our backs is much lighter at the end of our journey than when we started,
and that is the good news Jesus wants to share with us:
Your truth,
your new way of living
is never as heavy as your resistance to it.

X is for X Marks the Spot

Don't be afraid to start over.
This time, you're not starting from scratch.
You're starting from experience.
— KAREN SALMANSOHN, AUTHOR AND GRAPHIC ARTIST

The phrase "X marks the spot" brings two ideas to mind:

The first one is the *You are here* sign.

You are here.
X marks this spot.
This is where you are today.

"Do not worry about tomorrow for tomorrow will bring worries of its own," Jesus said.
"Today's trouble is enough for today."

You are here. Today.
Let go of yesterday's worries.
Don't worry about tomorrow's worries.
You are here, today, and this is your starting point.

I know, easier said than done. I *know!*

Nevertheless, you are here – on this day, in this now.

There will be new worries,
but there will be new opportunities for gratitude,
and for God to show up and do that God thing –
you know, the unexpected, the surprising,
the transforming –
the grace of it all.

You are here – X marks the spot.
And X marks the spot where grace is found.
No matter what you've done,
what you've said, who you've been,
from this spot,
this starting point,
you can be different.
You can do differently –
you can think and speak and relate to others differently.
With love, rather than fear.
With kindness, rather than mockery.
With mercy, rather than judgement.
There is nothing – and no one – anywhere, across time –
that says you are not allowed to change.
That says you are not allowed to learn and adjust and shift.
To do better,
and be better.

Here's my interpretation of Jesus' words about selling our possessions.
We can take it literally – get rid of all our stuff – but what if we,

here in the 21st century,
did it figuratively to start with?
What if this is our starting point for the bigger effort?

Consider that "possessions" also can be attitudes –
ways of thinking –
ways of relating to others.

What if we give up sexism and racism,
homophobia and xenophobia,
discrimination based on age and ability?

What if we give up intolerance, bigotry,
and "us versus them"?

What if we give up clinging to notions we know,
deep in our hearts,
are hurtful and harmful,
that we don't really want to believe any longer?

X marks the spot where you can begin –
you are here, today.
So worry about today – and who you are today.
X says it starts with you.

In her 2010 book *Thrift Store Saints: Meeting Jesus 25 Cents at a Time*, Jane Knuth writes about her experiences as a volunteer at a St. Vincent de Paul thrift store in Kalamazoo,

Michigan. It's a wonderful book about how helping others helps ourselves.
As the back of the book says, "Rather than viewing society's poor as problems to be solved, Jane begins to see them, one at a time, as saints who can lead us straight to the heart of Christ."

She wrote the following about the impact helping people living in poverty had on her:
"Gradually, over the first few months that I work there, it starts to become uneasily clear to me that we are not trying to change the world. We aren't trying to change poor people either. The only thing it seems we are trying to change is ourselves. This does not sit well with me. It is not enough. I am programmed to change the world. Changing myself seems pathetic in comparison."

But I've always believed we can't change the world until we first change ourselves.
We can't change the world
if the energy we put out is hurtful –
to ourselves and to others.
You are here.
This is your starting point.
Because without our offerings of our spirit and our energy, our faithfulness and our passion –
the world can't be changed.
We can't do the work of change if we keep those treasures to ourselves.

Which brings us to the second idea brought to mind by the phrase "X marks the spot": Treasure.
In literature, X marks the spot on a map where treasure is buried.
Treasure, or light –
whatever is hidden in sand or under a bushel
or inside a box at the back of a closet in the basement –
these are your talents, your skills,
your passion, your motivation –
and these are what the world needs.
It doesn't matter how small your world is –
your church or your neighbourhood
or a village on the other side of the globe –
if you are using your treasure and shining your light,
you are making a difference.

And that's the power of community –
particularly a community of faith –
that's one of the reasons, I think, we keep trying to maintain and hold on to and transform
our communities of faith –
we need others and we seek out those with whom we have values and goals in common.

Canadian film director and producer Deborah Day once said, "Connecting with those who love, like, and appreciate you restores the spirit and gives you energy to keep moving forward in this life."

This is so true. When we are with people whose spirits and ideas are in sync with ours, we feel energized and inspired and brave enough to try new activities and embrace new ideas.

When you change yourself, when you serve one person at a time and find yourself transformed by that interaction, you are starting to change yourself, and the world in which you live.

When Jesus says,
"The kingdom of heaven is like treasure which a man found and covered up. Then in his joy he goes and sells all that he has and buys that field,"
he also means the more you give away to others –
the more of your treasure you share with other people, the more of your light you shine on other people –
the better off you are.
Not just them, the people you are helping and supporting, but you too.

Because that's the kin-dom of God happening right there.
With every bit of your treasure that you share, every watt of light you shine,
with every thing you give up –
you are buying a field in the kin-dom of God right here, right now.

When you serve those who are struggling –
when you share your treasure with those who are in need –
when you shine your light on injustice and unfairness and inequality –
you are standing in the field of God –

(remember: God doesn't do castles and cathedrals, skyscrapers and mansions)

so you are standing in the field of God, a vast open space under a vast open sky –
maybe it's full of wildflowers, maybe it's full of wheat, maybe it's full of scruffy alder bushes –
but whatever, God's field is a wide, open space
full of possibilities and no limits –

and there you are, standing on your X.

The X that marks your spot –
your treasure –
your starting point for today.

And you are going to be outstanding.

Y IS FOR Yes

Say yes, and you'll figure it out afterwards.
— TINA FEY

When the world went into lockdown in the spring of 2020 because of the pandemic, I was able to provide worship online via a Facebook group, and broadcast from the sanctuary because my mother, Lynda, a pianist and former church music leader and choir director, lives with me.
We were isolated together
so we could provide the worship together,
and sing our hearts out in that empty sanctuary.

Providing church services online opened up my small, rural lay ministry to a whole whack of people across Canada, Florida (via our snowbird members), and England. Mostly, it let my friends and family in Ontario, where I lived before moving to Nova Scotia, see me in action.
Shalom!

One afternoon while I was in the middle of planning the worship for the letter Y, my friend Shelagh from Ontario phoned. Of course she asked what word I'd chosen for the penultimate worship in our Alphabet of Faith series. I told her that I'd originally chosen "Yearn" but had to change it because Mother kept hearing "urine."

In response, Shelagh suggested
Lynda take the morning off!
That made me laugh about having to sing *a cappella*,
and I said,
"No one's ready to hear me hit high D
without piano accompaniment."

Shelagh made a comment about the fact that I actually do this singing live,
really just putting it out there, adding, "You're generous in your vulnerability."
To which I responded, "That's a fine way of saying my singing sucks!"

But here are two things:
One, Mother wouldn't let me sing in public if I couldn't hold a tune.
And two, I don't care if my singing sucks because I'm simply grateful to be able to offer it.
I'm grateful I have enough confidence,
and an age-related acceptance of my weirdness,
as well as a deeply ingrained sense of service to others,
that allowed for us to continue singing familiar hymns during the new adventure
of online worship.
All because I am not afraid to make a fool of myself.

This is also known as more enthusiasm than skill.

No one likes making mistakes; no one likes doing something wrong.
No one sets out to make a fool of themselves.
Granted, I have lots of practice with it,
but that humility is one side of a coin –
the other side is confidence.
Not just in myself, but confidence in my faith family that allows me to be vulnerable.

What a blessing to my work, and to my spiritual life,
that I have never experienced a congregation as a hostile or toxic environment
where I couldn't be myself, or do what needed to be done, or not know how far I could push the envelope.
The places I've served as a lay worship leader have been welcoming, supportive, and encouraging.

The trust those congregations have in me, and that I have in them, allows me to be vulnerable –
to put myself out there with my thoughts and ideas as well as with my singing –
to do the best work I can in the hopes of providing the most meaningful worship I can.
It also allows me to challenge them with ideas that come from my heart –
and perhaps from that holy energy that flows in us and around us and between us.

So often, we let fear –
the knee-jerk reaction of "I can't" –
stop us from doing something new, different, challenging.
I've battled the pervasive influence of "I can't" for most of my life.
Fear holds us back from so much, keeps us in our comfort zone, in one place,
with a narrow view and a limited perspective.
Instead,
be brave so you can
be generous in your vulnerability.

Which is the absolute opposite of what our mind says.
Our mind says, "Wait! No! Don't do that! You'll screw up! You'll embarrass yourself!"
But our hearts say,
"Try it! What's the worst that can happen?"
Truly, the worst thing that can happen is your voice breaks on a high note,
or you miss your cue for the beginning of the hymn.
Who notices? Who remembers? Who cares?

According to sociologist Brené Brown, who actually wrote a book about vulnerability,
"The definition of vulnerability is uncertainty, risk, and emotional exposure. Vulnerability is not weakness; it is our greatest measure of courage."

The courage to sing.
The courage to write and share a message.
The courage to say yes.
To be a lay worship leader in the first place.
Me, of all people.
Shalom!

When Jesus says, *Love God*, we say *yes*.
When Jesus says, *Love one another*, we say *yes*.
When Jesus says, *Treat others as you want to be treated*, we say *yes*.
When Jesus says, *Love your enemies*, we say *yes*.
When Jesus says, *You are the light of the world*, we say *yes*.
When Jesus says, *Turn the other cheek, give up your coat as well, go another mile, help your neighbour*, we say *yes*.
When Jesus says, *Seek, knock, ask, pray, forgive, take the hard road, wash feet, break bread, build a bigger table*,
we say *yes*.

Remember what Jesus said *no* to?
The temptations of satisfied hunger, power, and wealth. In fact, whenever he was given the chance to back out of what he believed God wanted him to do, Jesus said *no*.

He said *yes* to God. He said *yes* to God's vision for his life and for the world. He said *yes* to his commitment to a new truth that would mean a new way of living.

He said *yes* to speaking out for peace, mercy, and justice,
even though it put his life at risk,
all so that we can say yes to the kin-dom of God. To that
new kind of community Jesus envisioned.

So why do we find it so hard to say yes
to Jesus' one commandment to love one another?
To treat others with kindness and mercy,
fairness and equality?
To be accepting and welcoming and – well, just *nice?*

Is it because we don't want to be vulnerable?
But remember what my wise friend Shelagh said:
You are generous in your vulnerability.

Generosity. Kindness. Mercy. Love.
All the things we get for an abundant life.
If we have to be a little bit vulnerable in order to say yes to all that –
to giving and receiving, to forgiving and redeeming –
Amen.
So be it.

Speaking of singing and songs,
the hymn I'd originally chosen
as the closing hymn for the letter Y
contains the word "slave."

This is also how we say yes to the kin-dom of God, my friends:

We recognize that the language we use and the behaviour we exhibit matters.
It says something about who we are –
and for us, that means who we are as people of God,
as followers of Jesus.

So we say yes to changing our language,
to recognizing that just because
"that's the way the song was originally written,"
using the word slave to mean servant,
doesn't make it right when we know better.
When God is asking us to *do* better.

We say yes to being aware, to being welcoming, and open, and understanding.
We say yes to a new way, and a new truth,
to a new way of living in that truth.
We say yes to Jesus.

Because the world needs more generosity,
more vulnerability,
more singing,
and more Jesus.

Z is for Zeal

*It takes courage to be considered, at times,
as a little too zealous.*
— F. D. VAN AMBURGH

Zeal is "great energy or enthusiasm in pursuit of a cause or an objective."

Energy and enthusiasm.

About 15 years ago, I came across an envelope containing my report cards from elementary school. I sat down to read through them and discovered what my Grade One teacher wrote in my mid-year report card: "Sara engages in physical activities with much enthusiasm but not a lot of skill."

First of all, who says that about a six-year-old kid? About Grade One gym??

However.
When I read those words as a 37-year-old woman,
I realized –
they are accurate. I've always been like that.
In fact, that's how I've lived my life:
With more enthusiasm than skill.

And those of you who know me personally know I have a lot of energy.

I am full of zeal.
Enthusiasm and energy in pursuit of a goal.

Who needs skill when you have zeal?
Who needs skill when you have enthusiasm and energy and passion?

Zeal is about living life fully and completely, with enthusiasm and excitement.
It's about being inspired and awakened.
It's about having a passion for life – for a goal, a cause, a project, a mission.

Zeal – enthusiasm, energy, excitement, passion – is necessary for a life of faith.

We can't live as a people of faith
if we aren't filled with zeal –
if we don't feel enthusiastic about it and energized by it.
Because even when we are tired, discouraged,
fretful, fearful –
if we have zeal, true enthusiasm and energy for the work we are called to do, it carries us over the rough patches, through the hard times, out of the dark valleys.

Let me just say, zeal sounds like joy –
big and loud and hyper, cheerful and happy
and, well, enthusiastic.
But just as joy can be quiet and gentle, zeal is simply that underlying passion that fuels our calling.
It doesn't have to be out there – because it's in our hearts.

And zeal is another way of speaking about passion.

We need to have a passion for our faith.
A passion for kindness, mercy, and justice.
A passion for peace and hope and compassion.
A passion for humility.
A passion for helping others.

Let's be clear at this moment:
We're not talking passion in the same sense as "the passion of Christ" in the last days of his life. That passion comes from the Latin verb for "suffering."

This passion is a zest for life.

Being passionate means being in tune with your spiritual life and being on the lookout for meaning.
It means being able to see answers to our questions and prayers even when they aren't what we want or hope for.
It means being able to find guidance in sudden appearances or sounds

or a quiet voice in the dark –
like my father, who died in 2009, whispering to me in the dark early one morning in January 2019: "Patience."
That word got me through a time of doubt and uncertainty and pandemic chaos.
Whenever I thought my life had lost its purpose, I whispered that word to myself
and didn't give up.
Breathe in, breathe out, have patience.
Be zealous in your patience.

As poet and graphic artist Morgan Harper Nichols says, "Having patience is the capacity to accept a slower pace as part of the bigger picture."

Being passionate means cherishing every moment
and not missing a thing,
or wasting a moment
(unless, of course, we are enjoying a rest – and a nap is never a wasted moment).

Elisabeth Kübler-Ross, a psychiatrist who specialized in dying and death, said, "It's only when we truly know and understand that we have a limited time on earth – and that we have no way of knowing when our time is up – that we will begin to live each day to the fullest as if it's the only one we had."

Death is a formidable reminder to pursue our passion, to live with peace and joy and love –
and enthusiasm! –
because when you are told you have only weeks to live, you don't want to realize you wasted your best years on resistance and procrastination,
on complaining,
on confrontations and grudges,
or worse, on hatred.

Being passionate about life means feeling a deep connection to other peoples, and to all living creatures – to all creation.
The mantra through the pandemic was "We are all in this together."
We experienced an incredible cultural and societal shift –
when we were faced with what it looks like to take care of each other regardless of age or gender or income,
to uphold each other regardless of race or ethnicity,
to stand together against greed and corruption and abuse of power.

Which brings us nicely to ...

Being passionate about life – and living –
means giving ourselves in service to the common good.
In service to those who are vulnerable –
the poor, the sick, the hungry, the meek.
In service to those who fight for justice and for peace.

In service to the many, not the few.

Being passionate about life means realizing that grace is the place where it all begins and ends.
Because grace is transformative, and allows us to see people and circumstances in new ways,
and is from the Spirit –
our zeal begins with grace and ends with grace.
No matter what we do, as long as we do it with love and in right relationship with God,
we are in a place of grace.

Here, in paraphrase, are verses 9–18 from chapter 12 of Paul's letter to the Romans:
"Be devoted to one another in love.
Honour one another above yourselves.
Share with people who are in need.
Practice hospitality.
Bless those who persecute you.
Rejoice with those who rejoice; mourn with those who mourn.
Live in harmony with one another.
Do not be proud, do not be conceited.
Be careful to do what is right in the eyes of everyone.
If it is possible, as far as it depends on you, *live at peace with everyone.*"

Such passion! Such zeal!

It's enough to make an introvert like me crawl back under the bed blankets.

But zeal doesn't have to mean loud and noisy,
enthusiasm and energy don't have to be overly enthusiastic or high energy.
Zeal isn't about being provocative or provoking.
It's not always about making as much noise as you can or about making the biggest gestures;
it's not about singing at the top of your voice and turning up the volume on the instruments.

Zeal is about finding what you are passionate about,
figuring out where your enthusiasm and energy flow to –
and following it.
Giving in to it – giving in to being passionate about life.
About your life, and about the lives of others.

When you're talking with your best friend,
what do you speak passionately about?
What makes her say,
"Whoa, you're really worked up about that?"
(and you are so grateful she's your BFF
because she isn't bowled over by this zeal
and doesn't hang up the phone
and laughs when you stop to take a breath).

Think of the one thing that makes you happy –
that makes you lose track of time when you do it –
the thing that you would do every day if you didn't have to be a caregiver
or clean the house or homeschool or go to a 12-hour shift at work.
What makes you happy? What are you passionate about?

Where your heart is,
there too is your treasure.
And your treasure is your offering to this world.
Your treasure –
your passion, your zeal, your energy, your spirit –
is what the world needs now.

AFTERWORD:
WORDS OF FAITH

"We're trying to build a gentler, kinder society and if we all pitch in – just a little bit – we're going to get there."
– ALEX TREBEK, host of *Jeopardy,*
from his final message to viewers
in January 2021

One afternoon, as the dog and I walked along a gravel road near my rural home, a man stopped his car to chat with us.
"I'm retarded now," he told me.
"You mean you're retired," I replied. No smile. No chuckle.
"Yep, I'm retarded," he insisted.

Sometimes it's painful to talk with people, isn't it?
They can be so obnoxious,
deliberately and provocatively so.
What he said wasn't amusing nor particularly clever, even though obviously he thought it was, and he wasn't going to be deterred by that politically-correct woman from down the road.
On the upside, he hasn't stopped to chat with me since.
He also won't have stopped believing there is nothing wrong with what he said.

Words are like seeds. They get planted in hearts and minds and they grow.

Do we want noxious weeds growing in those hearts and minds,
or do we want the wind-waved sweetness of wildflowers?

Words matter.
Every single word that comes out of our mouths or our pens or gets typed matters.
Because every single word lands in the eyes and ears of another human being.
In 2018, the words of Canada's national anthem were changed to be gender neutral. When "Thy sons command" changed back to "All of us command," the original lyrics of 1908, an older woman said to me, "I don't know why they changed the words. They don't bother me."

Those words don't bother me.
I've always sung it that way.
If it was good enough for my grandparents, it's good enough for me.

I tried to explain, but the concept of gender neutral, or inclusive, language, was lost on her.
By choice.

The words we speak and write are deliberate choices. We can choose to sing "Thy sons" – a double-whammy of archaic and male-oriented language – or we can choose to honour all the people who served, and serve, this country by singing "All of us." When I sing "All of us," I think of my husband's three maternal aunts who served as nurses during World War II.

The words we use matter.
Indian or Aboriginal.
Eskimo or Inuit.
First Nations and First Peoples.
Indigenous.

Every time the identifier for the first inhabitants of this continent is changed, there's a reason.
It's not done to be "politically correct" –
but to be culturally and historically accurate, and to be sensitive to the needs of others.

The needs of others to be recognized and respected and treated with dignity.

This is the intellectual evolution of humanity – this is how we respond to knowledge and understanding and acceptance. When we know better, we do better. The words we use reflect this.

A few years ago, I was in a play. The director wouldn't let one of the actors say the word "hell" in one of their lines; instead, the actor had to say, "H-E-double-hockey-sticks." But it was okay to use the word "cripple."

Another character, playing up a bad back, complained he was "doomed to be a cripple the rest of his life."
During rehearsals, this line bothered me,
but I didn't try to figure out why because I was the new member with a small role and there were more important things to worry about –
until our performances began and the hurtfulness of the word "cripple" took on real form.
Two of our four performances were attended by a person who used a wheelchair.

Some might say,
"What's wrong with the word 'cripple'?" and "If it's in the Bible, it's okay with me."

My response is:
Say it to the man in the wheelchair who attended the Friday night performance of the play.
Call him that to his face.
Tell the woman at the Thursday night performance to toughen up and not be hurt by the use of the word "cripple" to gain a laugh.

This isn't about being politically correct; it's about being socially correct, culturally correct, and morally correct.
It's about being kind and merciful and humble. It's about being mindful of the needs of others to be treated with respect and dignity.

I suspect, however, that those who roll their eyes
don't know someone who uses a wheelchair.
They don't know someone who is differently abled.
They don't know someone who will be hurt by words like
"cripple" and "retard" and "queer"
used as comedy, as put-downs.

Maybe they don't care.
Maybe they think the phrases, "Oh, I was just kidding,"
and "No offence, eh?" are enough to cover their ignorance.

Part of the reason we resist being called out on our use of words is that we hate to be wrong, but even more, we don't like being embarrassed.
No one likes to be shamed –
but you know what? It's not about us. It's not about our feelings.
Kindness, mercy, and justice start with a willingness to listen, and accept,
then change our language and behaviour.

Honestly, do we really want to hurt other people?
I'm tired of awareness and inclusivity being considered faults and weaknesses, rather than basic expectations.
I want kindness to be our default. I want acceptance to be our default.
I want us to be willing to listen to another person's perspective and have the decency to respect their experience and their feelings.

I want to be able to say, "Let's not use that word,"
without someone rolling their eyes.

I want awareness rather than defensiveness,
politeness rather than offensiveness,
decency rather than ignorance.
Is that really such a big ask?

The words we use as people of faith, then,
matter even more
because the language we use shapes our understanding.
We talk about love
but are we actually *speaking* with love? With peace? With humility? With fairness?
Do our words make everyone feel welcome and accepted and part of the community of faith?

In her new book *The Making of Biblical Womanhood*, Beth Allison Barr writes, "As a medieval historian, I know Christians translated Scripture in gender-inclusive ways long before the feminist movement." Barr goes on to explain that the way biblical texts were translated, many medieval people likely perceived gender-inclusive language as commonplace.

I was raised on inclusive language because of the young, progressive ministers – a husband and wife – at the church we attended in the 1970s.

I asked one of them, Dorothy Naylor, a diaconal minister now in her 80s, what she remembers about using inclusive language during worship back then.

Sadly, her strongest memories are those times when someone objected to it, such as referring to God as "she" on the Sunday that is Mother's Day. It's the single objections she remembers from the early years of her ministry, even though many people supported her work to make the words of hymns and scriptures and prayers more representative of all the members of the congregation.

Because of Dorothy's influence on my mother and my mother's role as music leader at women's conferences in the 1980s, I'm aggressively inclusive in my language, to the point I can alter the language used in a scripture reading on the fly – just like a medieval preacher!

It's a skill I'm proud of because I want the words coming out of my mouth to include every single person sitting in front of me.

Just because Jesus is recorded in some Bibles as using the term "Father" doesn't mean I have to.

Not in the 21st century, not when the world needs more Jesus.

Jesus was about radical inclusion – hey, this is the guy that tells us to love our enemies –
so I want love to include everyone,
which is why whenever I use the word "love," I always add,

"Where love is …
kindness, compassion, mercy, justice, peace, acceptance, welcome, tolerance, hospitality."

Because words matter,
and a big, all-encompassing word like love
(or God)
can be dismissed if we don't define it accurately
to ensure everyone is included.

In the words of Eston Williams, a now-retired United Methodist minister in rural Texas, when his congregation was voting on allowing same-sex marriages:
"I'd rather be excluded for who I include, than included for who I exclude."

After all, Jesus' two great commandments were
Love God
and
love your neighbour.
Plus that wee little add-on at the last minute: Be unified.

Be nice to each other. Help each other out.
Put up with each other.
Be kind. Be merciful. Be fair.
Be mindful of the needs of others.
Be radical in your inclusion
because
words matter.

We change people's minds one idea at a time,
one experience at a time,
one word at a time.

Shalom!

ACKNOWLEDGEMENTS

I am grateful and honoured to live and work in Mi'kma'ki, the traditional and unceded territory of the Mi'kmaq, a First Nations people of the Northeastern Woodlands, indigenous to the areas now known as Canada's Atlantic Provinces and the Gaspé Peninsula of Quebec as well as the northeastern region of Maine.

Thank you to Wood Lake Publishing editor Mike Schwartzentruber for his guidance on this manuscript and his fine-tuning of my ideas, and to author Donna Sinclair who helped get this manuscript into Mike's hands.

Many thanks to the congregation of Trinity United Church in Oxford, Nova Scotia, for its enthusiastic support of my lay ministry, and for not asking me to do extemporaneous prayer!

I'm also thankful for the members of the River Philip community of faith who provided my first opportunities to lead worship. I am who I am today because of those women.

F is for friendship and I couldn't get through this life without Sarah, Shelagh, Jennifer, Janice, Kerry, and Eleni, who are always there when I need a friend. Author, mentor, and friend Marjorie Simmins deserves a medal for her unflagging encouragement of my writing. Also, I'm very grateful for those friends of my Facebook author page who have remained faithful and supportive for so many years.

Speaking of the woman who truly is responsible for who I am, love and gratitude to my mother, whose room is down the hall from my office, so she hears all the noises coming out of that room when I work then listens after I flop down on her couch – thanks for the talk therapy and the retail therapy.

Last but not least, love, love, love to my husband, Dwayne Mattinson, who didn't really understand what he was getting into when he married that city girl from Ontario who is a writer. Thanks for feeding me, for doing the dishes, and for telling me again and again, "You can do it."

And I do it because of Jesus, who believed so wholeheartedly in our potential that it gives me the courage to use my skills – and my enthusiasm – to carry on his work.

ABOUT THE AUTHOR

SARA JEWELL is a long-time columnist, essayist, and freelance writer. Her work has appeared in newspapers and magazines across Canada since 1995. She started her writing career at the *United Church Observer* and continues to write for *Broadview*. She also writes for *Saltscapes* magazine.

Her magazine writing has been recognized by the Associated Church Press, the Canadian Church Press, the Atlantic Journalism Awards, the Atlantic Community Newspaper Awards, the International Regional Magazine Awards, and the Edna Staebler Personal Essay Contest.

Drawing from personal experience, extensive reading of contemporary Christian authors, and the critical issues and transformative events covered by the news, Sara's spiritual writing is built on the foundation of her belief that "the world needs more Jesus."

Sara is the author of the collection of essays, *Field Notes: A City Girl's Search for Heart and Home in Rural Nova Scotia*.

Born and raised in Ontario, Sara graduated from Queen's University with English and Education degrees. She worked as a radio newscaster in Ontario and Vancouver, and now works as a substitute teacher and lay worship leader for the United Church. She is currently enrolled in a certificate program for Thanatology, the study of death and bereavement.

Sara lives on the north shore of Nova Scotia with her husband, mother, a few pets, and a flock of chickens.

Connect with her online at www.sarajewell.ca and @JewellofaWriter

ALSO AVAILABLE FROM WOOD LAKE

The Voice of the Galilean

**THE STORY OF A LIFE, A JOURNEY,
A DISCOVERY, A GIFT, AND A FATE**

REX WEYLER

Rex Weyler's *The Voice of the Galilean* stands as one of the most clear, compelling, and concise tellings of the life and teachings of Jesus ever written. Excerpted and updated from his seminal book *The Jesus Sayings: The Quest for His Authentic Message* – a brilliant synthesis of the work of international Bible scholars and some 200 ancient sources, including the gospels of Thomas and Mary – *The Voice of the Galilean* distills the teachings of Jesus with crystal clarity, sensitivity, insight, and passion. Equally important, Weyler challenges readers to bear "witness" to Jesus' message today, in their own lives.

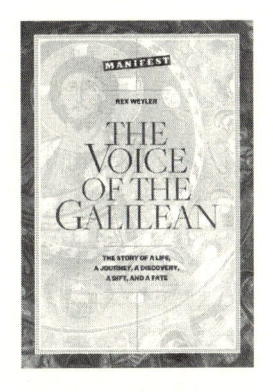

ISBN 978-1-77343-155-0
96 PAGES, 4.25" X 6.25" PAPERBACK, $12.95

WOOD LAKE

Imagining, living, and telling
the faith story.

WOOD LAKE IS THE FAITH STORY COMPANY.

It has told
- the story of the seasons of the earth, the people of God, and the place and purpose of faith in the world;
- the story of the faith journey, from birth to death;
- the story of Jesus and the churches that carry his message.

Wood Lake has been telling stories for more than 35 years. During that time, it has given form and substance to the words, songs, pictures, and ideas of hundreds of storytellers.

Those stories have taken a multitude of forms – faith curricula, parables, poems, drawings, prayers, epiphanies, songs, books, paintings, hymns, and more – all driven by a common mission of serving those on the faith journey.

WOOD LAKE PUBLISHING INC.
485 Beaver Lake Road, Kelowna, BC, Canada v4v 1s5
250.766.2778

www.woodlake.com